SOUTHERN AFRICA
AN ECONOMIC PROFILE

J du Toit and AJ Jacobs

ABSA BANK

Southern Book Publishers (Pty) Ltd

The information and opinions contained in this document have been compiled or arrived at from sources believed to be reliable and in good faith, but no representation or warranty, expressed or implied, is made by the authors or ABSA Bank. All opinions expressed herein are those of the authors and subject to change without notice.

ISBN 1 86812 649 8

First edition, first impression 1995

Published by
Southern Book Publishers (Pty) Ltd
PO Box 3103, Halfway House, 1685

Cover design by Alix Gracie

Set in New Baskerville 8/10 point
by Adcorp Graphics

Printed and bound by Creda, Transvaal.

Table of contents

Introduction

Over the years economic and social development in Africa has been adversely affected by a variety of factors such as international business cycles, natural disasters (droughts and floods), a heavy foreign debt burden, a lack of physical infrastructure, and political and civil strife.

Despite these factors, a number of African countries have made substantial progress in recent years in addressing the structural bottlenecks and financial imbalances that constrained their growth potential, while others are still confronted by serious and difficult economic, financial, and in some cases, political problems. The continent is, however, rich in metal and mineral resources, which are still in great demand by the rest of the world. Its natural beauty and wildlife attract large numbers of tourists each year, which earns African countries large amounts of much needed foreign exchange.

The countries in Southern Africa are no exception. For the purpose of this booklet, Southern Africa comprises Angola, Botswana, Kenya, Lesotho, Madagascar, Malawi, Mauritius, Mozambique, Namibia, South Africa, Swaziland, Tanzania, Zaire, Zambia and Zimbabwe.

Positive developments in Southern Africa during recent years have led to a growing need for greater economic integration and cooperation among the countries in the region. Political transformation and stability, economic reform and social upliftment will hopefully change the face of the region for the better.

Being the region's most advanced and dynamic economy, South Africa's participation is widely viewed as of vital importance to the successful economic integration and transformation of the Southern African countries. The transition of South Africa to a multiparty democracy in 1994 eliminated a major stumbling block in this respect.

As proof of this, South Africa has since become a member of the Southern African Development Community (SADC). The country still has to become a member of the African, Caribbean and Pacific (ACP) group of 70 developing countries under the Lomé Convention. An economic grouping of 30 Indian Ocean Rim (IOR) countries, comprising South and East Africa, South and East Asia, the Middle East, and Australia, also seems a future possibility. South Africa will undoubtedly be an important member of such a group of countries.

It is against this background that this concise reference work of key features and statistics on Southern Africa is published – having placed South Africa within the context of Southern Africa. The country has at its disposal agricultural, industrial, financial, research and technological knowledge and experience, as well as a well-established economic infrastructure which can be of great value to the other countries in the region.

The analysis starts with South Africa compared to the Southern African region, the African continent and the world as a whole, based on various indicators. This is followed by a broad overview of the 15 countries within the region, and developments on the political, social and economic fronts. In conclusion, the region's natural resources and environmental aspects are analysed.

The authors are deeply indebted to the Africa Institute of South Africa, based in Pretoria, for providing a substantial part of the information presented in this booklet. The assistance and cooperation of the staff at the Institute are greatly appreciated. The contributions of Miss SJ Dreyer for compiling the graphs and Mrs IH Lindsay-Smith for secretarial services are gratefully acknowledged.

Symbols used in the tables:

– indicates nil or negligible

.. indicates data is not available or not applicable

The contents were finalised during July 1995.

The Authors

1 South Africa in a global, continental and regional context

Africa has 53 independent states, 47 of which are on the continent and 6 of which are islands. There are 33 coastal countries and 15 landlocked countries. Of these 15 landlocked countries, 6 are within the Southern African region. Southern Africa, and thus South Africa, plays an important role in Africa, as is evident from the information provided in this section.

Africa's total surface area is 22,3% of that of the world, but only 12,7% of the world's population live in Africa. As a result, Africa's population density is 24 persons per km², compared to 42 persons per km² for the world as a whole. Southern Africa's population density is only 19 persons per km², and in South Africa it is even lower at 11 persons per km². Furthermore, only 19 African countries have a population of more than 10 million people. In Southern Africa, 8 countries have a population of more than 10 million people, and only Zaire and South Africa have more than 40 million people.

Most countries in Africa are relatively small. Thirty-one have an area of far less than 500 000 km² – roughly the size of Spain – while there are a few that are among the largest countries in the world. In Southern Africa, 10 of the 15 countries are larger than 500 000 km², with South Africa making up 11,7% of the region's total surface area.

The world's arable land area is 11%, while that of Africa is only 6% – the smallest of all the continents (except for Oceania). The arable land area in Southern Africa is about 7% (excluding Mauritius, where it is more than 50%). These figures illustrate why famine is a major problem in many African countries. South Africa's arable land area of 11%, and the modern agricultural methods employed, are the major reasons why the country is largely self-sufficient regarding food production.

TABLE 1.1: BASIC INDICATORS

	World	Africa	Southern Africa	South Africa
Surface area ('000 km²)	136 000,0	30 328,7	10 446,5	**1 220,9**
Population (million, 1995)	5 712,0	725,0	223,6	**43,5**
Urbanisation (% of population, 1995)	48	37	40	**62**
Total fertility rate (1992)	3,1	5,7	5,6	**4,1**
Life expectancy (years, 1992)	66	54	54	**63**
Infant mortality (per 1 000 live births, 1992)	60	89	87	**53**
Crude birth rate (per 1 000 population, 1992)	25	41	41	**31**
Crude death rate (per 1 000 population, 1992)	9	14	13	**9**
Country credit rating (%, March 1995)	38,1	21,5	25,0	**42,5**
Total GNP ($ billion, 1993)	24 257	433	169	**118**
Composition of GDP (%, 1992):				
• Agriculture	..	19	29	**4**
• Industry (including mining)	..	34	29	**42**
• Services	..	47	42	**54**
Electricity supply (1991):				
• Net maximum capacity of generating plant (MW)	2 856 158	84 503	49 181	**39 905**
• Production (GWh)	12 006 581	309 515	186 287	**155 812**
Motor vehicles ('000, 1990)	578 400	13 300	6 779	**5 100**

Sources: Africa Institute, Eskom, Institutional Investor

1.1 Expected population growth
(annual average for 1995 – 2000)

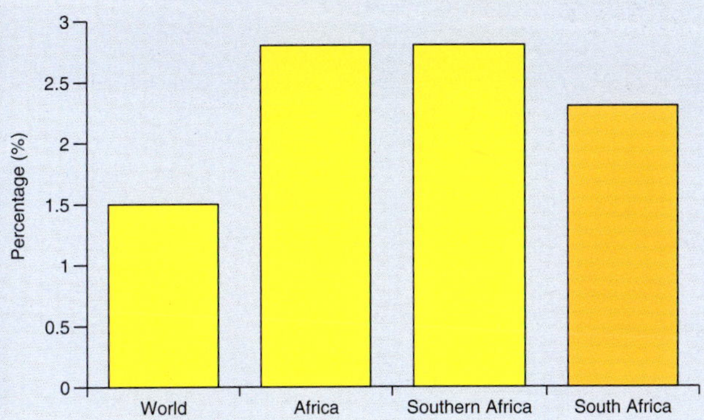

SOURCES: AFRICA INSTITUTE, WORLD BANK

1.2 Expected growth in urbanisation
(annual average for 1995 – 2000)

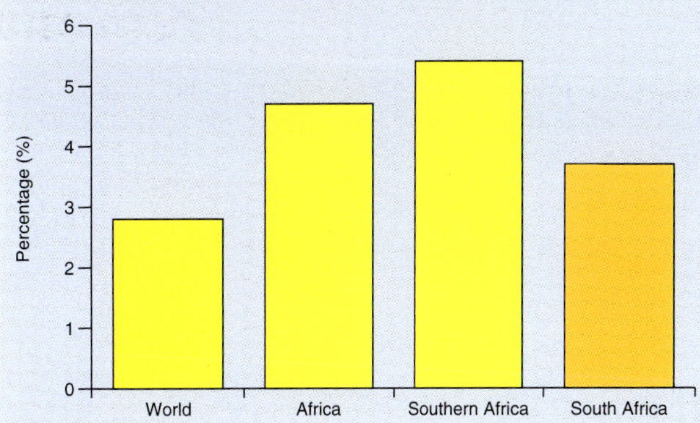

SOURCE: AFRICA INSTITUTE

1.3 Median age of population
(1995)

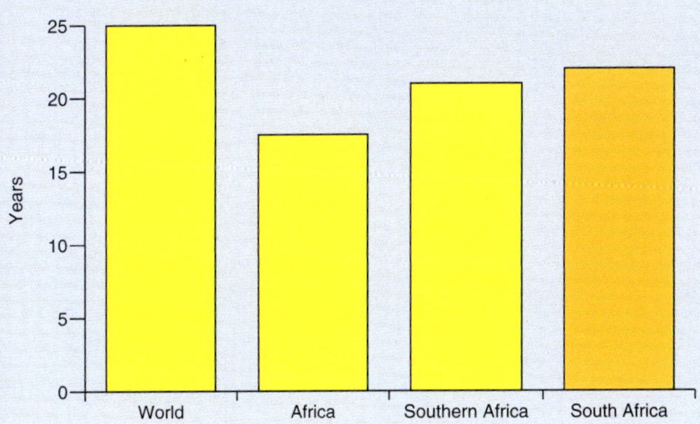

SOURCE: AFRICA INSTITUTE

1.4 Population per doctor
(1990)

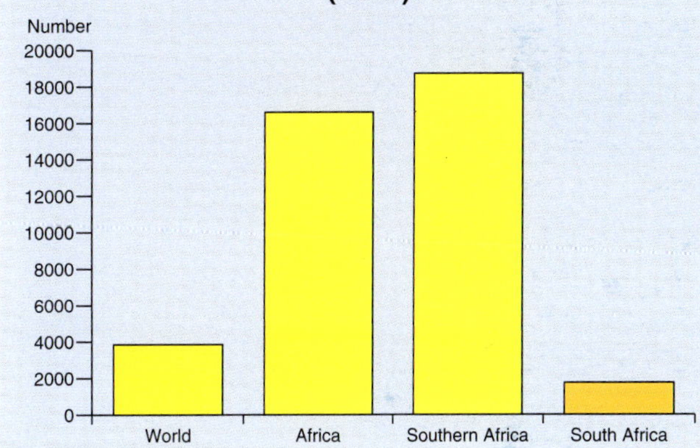

SOURCE: AFRICA INSTITUTE

1.5 GNP per capita
(1993)

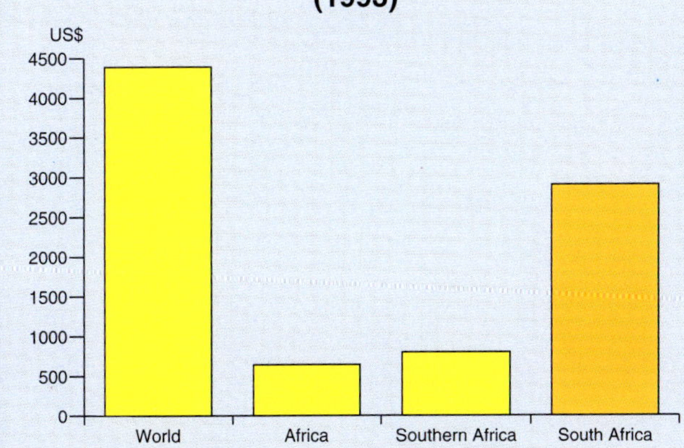

SOURCE: AFRICA INSTITUTE

1.6 Real GDP growth
(annual average for 1980 – 92)

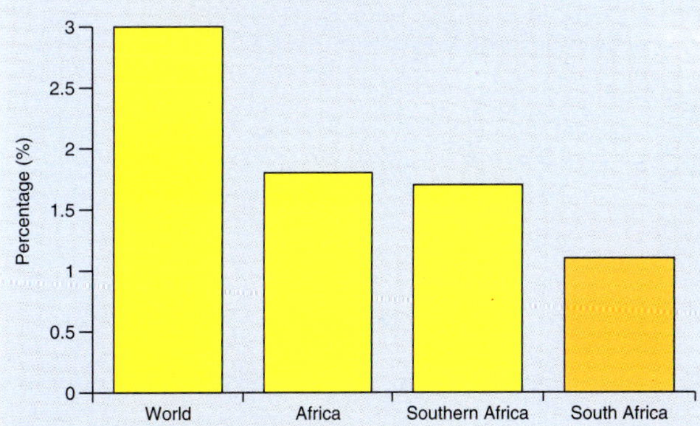

SOURCES: AFRICA INSTITUTE, WORLD BANK

2 The countries in Southern Africa: A broad overview

The emphasis on human rights and democratisation in Southern Africa is now being replaced by an awareness of the need to boost economic growth. Two important economic groupings have been formed in Africa: the Southern African Development Community (SADC), of which South Africa became a member in August 1994, and the Common Market for Eastern and Southern Africa (COMESA), which includes nine of the 11 SADC countries. South Africa's well-developed economic infrastructure, agricultural, industrial and financial sectors, advanced technology, research institutions and medical facilities make it one of the most important countries in the region. As a result, closer cooperation on all fronts between South Africa and the other countries in the region is foreseen.

Southern Africa has been devastated by above-average drought cycles since the early 1980s, which had a major adverse effect on economic performance and social development in the region. Examining the statistics in table 2.1 regarding the percentage of arable land in each country, it is obvious that food production on a large scale can be problematic. Over the years South Africa has played a major role in famine relief and agricultural development in the subcontinent and will undoubtedly continue to do so.

TABLE 2.1: GENERAL BACKGROUND INFORMATION

	Surface area '000 km^2	Coastline km	% Arable land 1991	Capital and principal international airport	Official language(s)
Zaire	2 344,9	37	3	Kinshasa	French
Angola[1]	1 246,7	1 600	3	Luanda	Portuguese
South Africa[1]	**1 220,9**	**2 968**	**11**	**Pretoria/Cape Town[2]**	[6]
Tanzania[1]	945,1	1 424	6	Dar es Salaam/ Dodoma[3]	English/Swahili
Namibia[1]	824,3	1 528	1	Windhoek	English
Mozambique[1]	801,6	2 470	4	Maputo	Portuguese
Zambia[1]	752,6	landlocked	7	Lusaka	English
Madagascar	587,0	4 828	5	Antananarivo	French/Malagasy
Kenya	582,6	536	4	Nairobi	English/Swahili
Botswana[1]	581,7	landlocked	2	Gaborone	English/Tswana
Zimbabwe[1]	390,8	landlocked	7	Harare	English
Malawi[1]	118,5	landlocked	18	Lilongwe	English/Chewa
Lesotho[1]	30,4	landlocked	11	Maseru	English/South Sotho
Swaziland[1]	17,4	landlocked	12	Mbabane[4]	English/Swazi
Mauritius	2,0	177	52	Port Louis[5]	English/French

[1]Member of the SADC
Principal international airport: [2]Johannesburg; [3]Dar es Salaam; [4]Manzini; [5]Plaisance
[6]Afrikaans, English, Ndebele, North Sotho, South Sotho, Swazi, Tsonga, Tswana, Venda, Xhosa, Zulu

Source: Africa Institute

2.1 Africa

Madeira (Port)
RABAT
ALGIERS
TUNIS
TUNISIA
MOROCCO
Canary Islands (Sp)
TRIPOLI
MEDITERRANEAN SEA
El Aaiun
WESTERN SAHARA
ALGERIA
LIBYA
CAIRO
EGYPT
Tropic of Cancer
RED SEA
MAURITANIA
CAPE VERDE
NOUAKCHOTT
PRAIA
DAKAR
SENEGAL
BANJUL
GAMBIA
BISSAU
GUINEA BISSAU
MALI
NIGER
CHAD
ERITREA
ASMARA
KHARTOUM
SUDAN
Socotra (Yemen)
GULF OF ADEN
BAMAKO
NIAMEY
BURKINA FASO
OUAGADOUGOU
CONAKRY
GUINEA
FREETOWN
SIERRA LEONE
NIGERIA
ABUJA
NDJAMENA
DJIBOUTI
ADDIS ABABA
ETHIOPIA
CÔTE D'IVOIRE
YAMOUSSOUKRO
MONROVIA
LIBERIA
GHANA
TOGO
BENIN
Lagos
ABIDJAN
ACCRA
LOME
PORTO NOVO
CAMEROON
CENTRAL AFRICAN REPUBLIC
SOMALIA
BANGUI
MALABO
EQUATORIAL GUINEA
YAOUNDE
UGANDA
MOGADISHU
Equator
SAO TOME & PRINCIPE
SAO TOME
LIBREVILLE
KAMPALA
KENYA
INDIAN OCEAN
Annobon (E.G.)
GABON
CONGO
ZAIRE
RWANDA
KIGALI
NAIROBI
BRAZZAVILLE
BUJUMBURA
BURUNDI
KINSHASA
TANZANIA
Pemba
Zanzibar
VICTORIA
Cabinda (Ang)
DODOMA
DAR ES SALAAM
SEYCHELLES
Ascension (UK)
ATLANTIC OCEAN
LUANDA
MORONI
COMOROS
ANGOLA
MALAWI
Mayotte (Fr)
ZAMBIA
LILONGWE
LUSAKA
St Helena (UK)
HARARE
ZIMBABWE
MOZAMBIQUE
MADAGASCAR
ANTANANARIVO
NAMIBIA
MAURITIUS
WINDHOEK
BOTSWANA
PORT LOUIS
Mozambique Channel
Reunion (Fr)
GABORONE
Tropic of Capricorn
PRETORIA
MAPUTO
MBABANE
SWAZILAND
MASERU
LESOTHO
SOUTH AFRICA
INDIAN OCEAN
CAPE TOWN

3 Political developments

Southern Africa is in a phase of political transformation, as is evident from the independence of Namibia in 1990 and the democratic elections held in Malawi, Mozambique, South Africa and Zambia. Political progress, although slow, is being made in Angola, a country finally moving towards an end to years of civil war, and hopefully a sustainable political solution. Multiparty political systems have been adopted by most countries in the region. These political changes are helping to make the region more attractive to foreign investors.

Civil war in Zimbabwe and Namibia during the seventies and eighties, but especially in Mozambique and Angola until recently, has destroyed infrastructure, increased poverty and caused enormous health problems and social disorder. Landlocked countries in the region had to direct their foreign trade through other ports (mainly those in South Africa) at great cost. The external trade of countries in a state of war was disrupted, while growth in fixed investment was extremely low, or even negative. This caused major economic problems in these countries.

South Africa held its first fully democratic election in April 1994, after which a government of national unity was formed by the three main political parties. The African National Congress (ANC) has the majority of seats in the government (63%), followed by the National Party (NP) with 20,5%, the Inkatha Freedom Party (IFP) with 10,8%, and the rest with a combined 5,7%. The other countries in the region, and especially the "Frontline states", have since fully accepted South Africa back within their ranks.

TABLE 3.1: POLITICAL INDICATORS

	Year of self-government	Date of independence	Status of country		Present leader(s)	
			Pre-independence	Present	Name	Since
Angola	..	11 November 1975	Portuguese colony 1891-1951 Portuguese province 1951-75	Unitary republic	Pres Jose Eduardo dos Santos	1979
Botswana	1965	30 September 1966	British protectorate 1895-1931 British High Commission Territory 1931-66	Unitary republic	Pres (Sir) Ketumile Masire	1980
Kenya	1963	12 December 1963	British colony 1895-1963	Unitary republic	Pres Daniel Arap Moi	1978
Lesotho	1965	4 October 1966	British protectorate 1868-84 British colony 1884-1931 British High Commission Territory 1931-66	Unitary monarchy	King Moshoeshoe II PM Ntsu Mokhehle	1995 1993
Madagascar	1958	26 June 1960	French colony 1896-1960	Unitary republic	Pres (Dr) Albert Zafy	1993
Malawi	1963	6 July 1964	British protectorate 1891-1964	Unitary republic	Pres Bakili Muluzi	1994
Mauritius	1967	12 March 1968	British colony 1810-1968	Unitary republic	Pres Cassam Uteem PM (Sir) Aneerood Jugnauth	1992 1982
Mozambique	..	25 June 1975	Portuguese colony 1881-1951 Portuguese province 1951-75	Unitary republic	Pres Joaquim Chissano	1986
Namibia	1985	21 March 1990	German protectorate 1884-1915 South African administration 1915-89 Joint South African and UN administration 1989-90	Unitary republic	Pres Sam Nujoma	1990
South Africa	**..**	**31 May 1910**	**Four British colonies formed autonomous Union of South Africa 1910**	**Unitary republic**	**Pres Nelson R Mandela**	**1994**
Swaziland	1967	6 September 1968	British protectorate 1902-31 British High Commission Territory 1931-68	Unitary monarchy	Queen Mother Lathwala Ntombi King Mswati III	1983 1986
Tanzania	1961	9 December 1961	German protectorate 1885-1919 British administration after World War I UN Trust Territory 1946-61	Unitary republic	Pres Ali Hassan Mwinyi	1985
Zaire	..	30 June 1960	Belgian colony 1885-1960	Unitary republic	Pres Mobutu Sese Seko	1970
Zambia	1964	24 October 1964	British protectorate 1924-64	Unitary republic	Pres Frederick Chiluba	1991
Zimbabwe	1923	18 April 1980	Self-governing British colony 1923-79 Unilaterally independent 1965-79 British interim control 1979-80	Unitary republic	Pres Robert G Mugabe	1987

Source: Africa Institute

3.1 Transformation to democracy

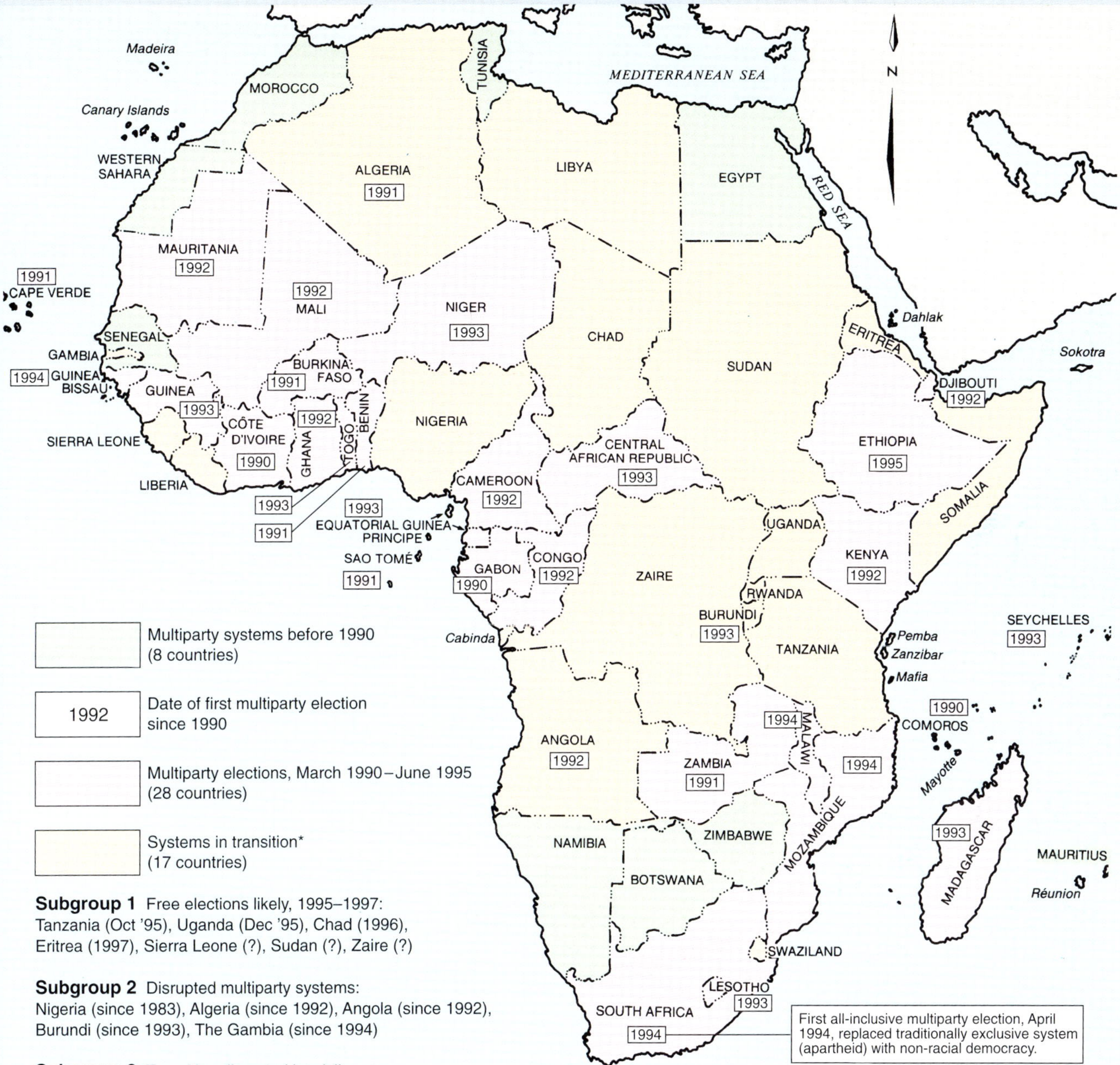

Multiparty systems before 1990 (8 countries)

1992 — Date of first multiparty election since 1990

Multiparty elections, March 1990–June 1995 (28 countries)

Systems in transition* (17 countries)

Subgroup 1 Free elections likely, 1995–1997: Tanzania (Oct '95), Uganda (Dec '95), Chad (1996), Eritrea (1997), Sierra Leone (?), Sudan (?), Zaire (?)

Subgroup 2 Disrupted multiparty systems: Nigeria (since 1983), Algeria (since 1992), Angola (since 1992), Burundi (since 1993), The Gambia (since 1994)

Subgroup 3 Transition disrupted by civil war: Liberia (since 1990), Somalia (since 1990), Rwanda (since 1994)

* In Libya and Swaziland there has been relatively little effective challenge to the non-party systems that have been entrenched since 1977 and 1973 respectively. While new constitutions are being written in Uganda and Sudan, there is an official preference in these countries for non-party systems.

4 Demographic developments

Africa has experienced rapid population growth since the mid-1960s, Southern Africa being no exception. The average annual population growth in the region is currently around 3%. Population growth in most Southern African countries is expected to be somewhat lower during the period 1995-2000 compared to 1990-95, but in a few cases – Angola, Mozambique and Tanzania – it is set to accelerate even further. A population growth rate of 2,3% per annum is projected for South Africa during 1995-2000, the same as in 1990-95.

At present, only 37% of the people living in Africa are urbanised. In some Southern African countries – Botswana, Kenya, Lesotho, Mozambique, Swaziland and Zambia – population growth in urban areas was more than double that of the total population in these countries during certain periods. The average annual rate of urbanisation is expected to still exceed population growth in all the Southern African countries during 1995-2000. South Africa's urban population is expected to increase by 3,7% per annum from 1995 to 2000, compared to 3,5% per annum during the 1980s.

Although AIDS is expected to have an impact on demographic trends in Africa in years to come, it will probably not cause the size of the total population to decline. Countries with high numbers of reported AIDS cases are mostly in Central and Southern Africa. According to a population study by the United Nations on the impact of AIDS, it is estimated that the total population in Central and Southern Africa will be 2,8% (7,3 million) less in the year 2000 and 4% (12,4 million) less in the year 2005 than it would have been in the absence of AIDS.

TABLE 4.1: POPULATION AND URBANISATION TRENDS

	1960		1995		2000		2010	
	Number millions	% urban	Number millions	% urban	Number millions	% urban	Number millions	% urban
Zaire	17,80	22	43,50	42	50,00	46	65,00	54
South Africa	**16,00**	**47**	**43,50**	**62**	**48,40**	**65**	**57,50**	**73**
Tanzania	10,20	5	28,50	40	33,30	46	44,50	54
Kenya	8,20	7	28,75	28	34,00	32	46,00	40
Mozambique	6,55	4	18,00	34	21,00	41	28,00	50
Madagascar	5,50	11	13,50	27	15,50	31	20,00	39
Angola	4,50	10	11,50	32	13,50	36	18,00	44
Zimbabwe	3,60	13	11,20	31	12,50	35	14,80	43
Malawi	3,40	4	10,00	14	11,50	16	15,00	21
Zambia	3,20	17	9,50	55	11,00	59	14,30	65
Lesotho	0,90	3	2,00	24	2,30	28	2,80	35
Mauritius	0,70	33	1,13	41	1,20	42	1,30	47
Namibia	0,60	15	1,60	31	1,85	34	2,45	42
Botswana	0,50	2	1,55	35	1,80	42	2,40	53
Swaziland	0,35	4	0,95	39	1,10	44	1,50	52

Source: Africa Institute

TABLE 4.2: POPULATION OF MAJOR CITIES (1995)

City	Country	Population '000	City	Country	Population '000
Kinshasa	Zaire	4 400	**PE/Uitenhage**	**South Africa**	**950**
Johannesburg[1]	**South Africa**	**2 500**	Beira	Mozambique	900
Cape Town[2]	**South Africa**	**2 400**	Bulawayo	Zimbabwe	750
Dar es Salaam	Tanzania	2 300	Mombasa	Kenya	600
Luanda	Angola	2 300	Blantyre	Malawi	500
Maputo	Mozambique	2 300	Lilongwe	Malawi	400
Nairobi	Kenya	2 000	Dodoma	Tanzania	350
Durban[3]	**South Africa**	**1 800**	Windhoek	Namibia	200
Antananarivo	Madagascar	1 700	Port Louis	Mauritius	200
Harare	Zimbabwe	1 700	Gaborone	Botswana	180
Lusaka	Zambia	1 300	Maseru	Lesotho	180
Pretoria	**South Africa**	**1 200**	Manzini	Swaziland	100

[1]Including Randburg, Sandton and Soweto
[2]Including Cape Peninsula and Cape Flats
[3]Including Kwamashu, Pinetown and Umlazi

Source: Africa Institute

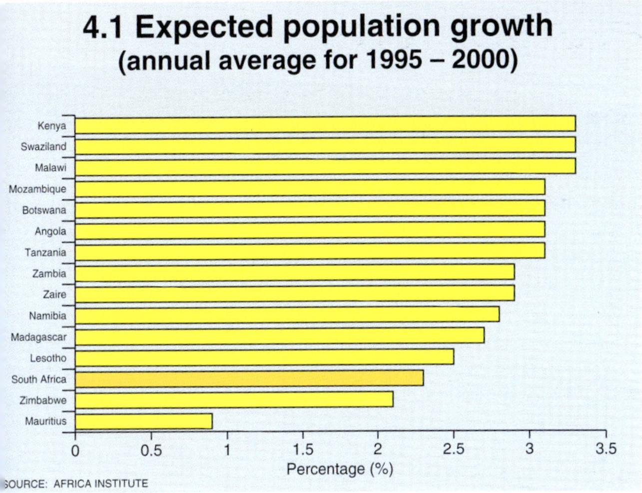
4.1 Expected population growth
(annual average for 1995 – 2000)
Kenya
Swaziland
Malawi
Mozambique
Botswana
Angola
Tanzania
Zambia
Zaire
Namibia
Madagascar
Lesotho
South Africa
Zimbabwe
Mauritius
0
0.5
1
1.5
2
2.5
3
3.5
Percentage (%)
SOURCE: AFRICA INSTITUTE

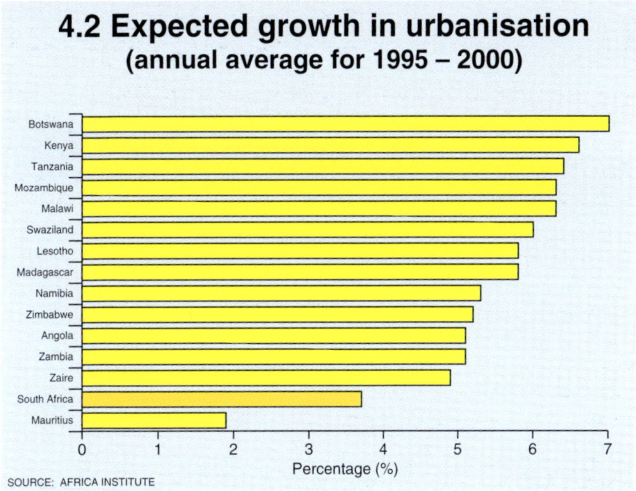
4.2 Expected growth in urbanisation
(annual average for 1995 – 2000)
Botswana
Kenya
Tanzania
Mozambique
Malawi
Swaziland
Lesotho
Madagascar
Namibia
Zimbabwe
Angola
Zambia
Zaire
South Africa
Mauritius
0
1
2
3
4
5
6
7
Percentage (%)
SOURCE: AFRICA INSTITUTE

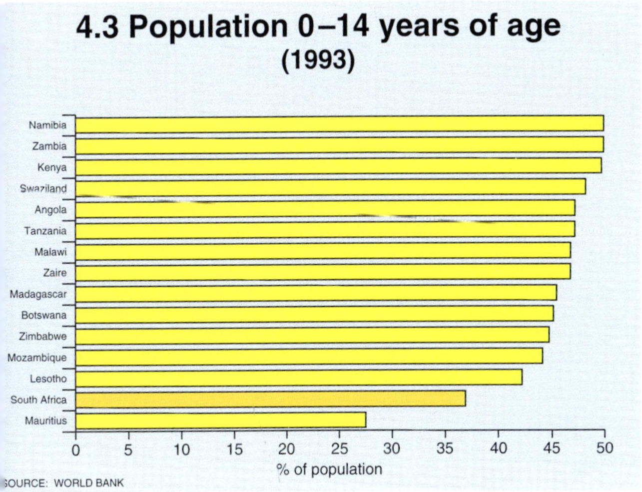
4.3 Population 0–14 years of age
(1993)
Namibia
Zambia
Kenya
Swaziland
Angola
Tanzania
Malawi
Zaire
Madagascar
Botswana
Zimbabwe
Mozambique
Lesotho
South Africa
Mauritius
0
5
10
15
20
25
30
35
40
45
50
% of population
SOURCE: WORLD BANK

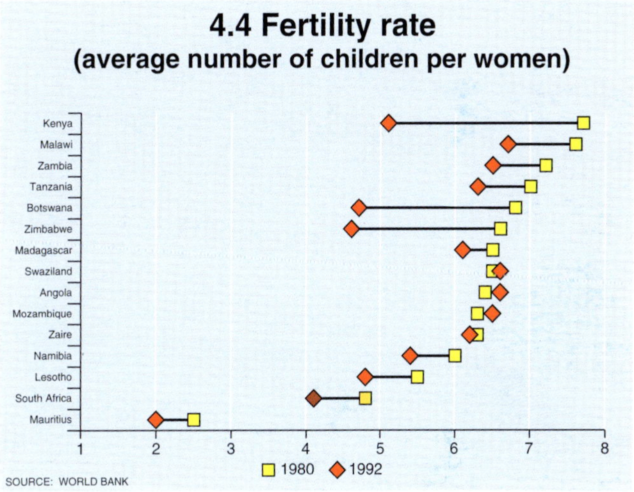
4.4 Fertility rate
(average number of children per women)
Kenya
Malawi
Zambia
Tanzania
Botswana
Zimbabwe
Madagascar
Swaziland
Angola
Mozambique
Zaire
Namibia
Lesotho
South Africa
Mauritius
1
2
3
4
5
6
7
8
1980
1992
SOURCE: WORLD BANK

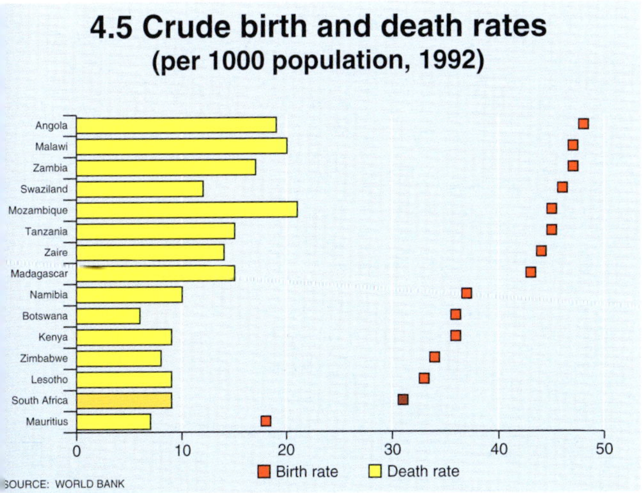
4.5 Crude birth and death rates
(per 1000 population, 1992)
Angola
Malawi
Zambia
Swaziland
Mozambique
Tanzania
Zaire
Madagascar
Namibia
Botswana
Kenya
Zimbabwe
Lesotho
South Africa
Mauritius
0
10
20
30
40
50
Birth rate
Death rate
SOURCE: WORLD BANK

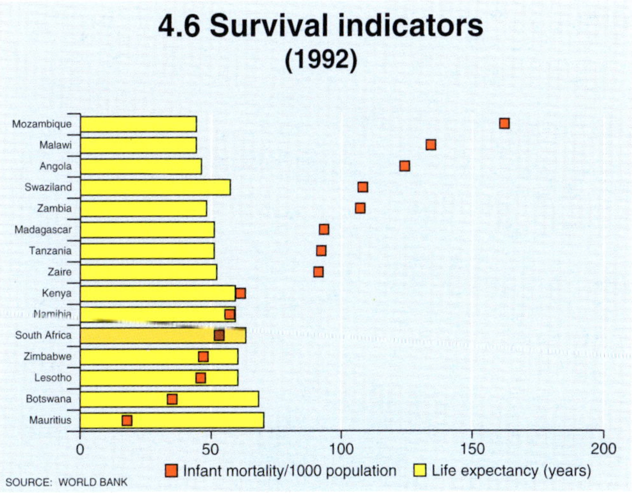
4.6 Survival indicators
(1992)
Mozambique
Malawi
Angola
Swaziland
Zambia
Madagascar
Tanzania
Zaire
Kenya
Namibia
South Africa
Zimbabwe
Lesotho
Botswana
Mauritius
0
50
100
150
200
Infant mortality/1000 population
Life expectancy (years)
SOURCE: WORLD BANK

5 Social and wealth profile

The above-average drought spells which occurred in Southern Africa during the 1980s and the early 1990s, as well as the continued high population growth, caused the average annual food production per capita to decline in virtually all the countries in the region. The only exceptions were Kenya and Mauritius, which recorded small increases of just 0,1% and 0,8% per annum respectively. The average annual food production per capita declined by 5% in Malawi, 3,3% in Zimbabwe, 3,1% in Botswana, 2,5% in Namibia, 2,2% in Lesotho and 2,1% in South Africa during the period 1979-92.

South Africa's relatively poor GNP per capita growth compared to other Southern African countries during 1985-93 (see graph 5.2) can be contributed to inter alia protracted drought cycles, weak commodity prices, and fierce international sanctions against the country during this period.

South Africa's electricity consumption per capita (3 901 kWh) was the highest in the Southern African region during the early 1990s, followed by Namibia with 1 257 kWh per capita. Seven of the 15 countries in the region have a per capita electricity consumption of well above the 466 kWh average for the whole of Africa. Madagascar has the lowest corresponding figure in the Southern African region (46 kWh), followed by Malawi with 54 kWh per capita.

The Human Development Index, as represented in graph 5.1, is a composite index of three basic factors of human development: longevity, knowledge and standard of living. Longevity is measured by life expectancy. Knowledge is measured by a combination of adult literacy (two-thirds) and mean years of schooling (one-third). Standard of living is measured by purchasing power, based on real GDP per capita adjusted for the local cost of living in each country.

TABLE 5.1: STANDARD OF LIVING INDICATORS

	GNP per capita US$ 1993	Newspaper copies per 1 000 people 1992	Radios per 1 000 people 1992	Television sets per 1 000 people 1992	Telephones per 1 000 people 1991	Passenger vehicles per 1 000 people 1991	Commercial vehicles per 1 000 people 1991
Mauritius	3 030	73	360	218	72[1]	34	13
South Africa	**2 980**	**31**	**304**	**98**	**144**	**99**	**44**
Botswana	2 790	13	122	17	43	12	19
Namibia	1 820	136	127	21	48	29	31
Swaziland	1 050	15	163	20	24	27	29
Angola	970[1]	12	29	6	8	12	4
Lesotho	650	8	33	6	12	4	..
Zimbabwe	520	18	84	27	31	23	8
Zambia	380	8	82	26	12	12	8
Kenya	270	14	87	10	15[1]	6	6
Madagascar	220	4	200	20	5[1]	4	3
Malawi	200	2	221	..	6	2	1
Zaire	210[2]	3	97	1	1	3	2
Tanzania	90	8	25	2	6[1]	2	2
Mozambique	90	5	47	3	4	6	2

[1]1990; [2]1991

Sources: Africa Institute, Euromoney, World Bank

TABLE 5.2: EDUCATION AND HEALTH INDICATORS

	Mean number of years schooling of population over age 25 1992			Enrolled pupils and students as % of age group 1991-92			Population per doctor 1990	% of children (0-1) immunised against tuberculosis 1993	Cumulative AIDS cases reported per 100 000 population 1993/94
	Total	Female	Male	Primary 5-12	Secondary 12-18	Tertiary 18-24			
Mauritius	4,1	3,3	4,9	106	54	2	1 200	99	1,6
South Africa	**3,9**	**3,7**	**4,1**	**109**	**71**	**14**	**1 750**	**66**	**8,1**
Swaziland	3,8	3,4	4,1	115	48	4	18 800	98	50,7
Lesotho	3,5	4,1	2,8	107	25	3	18 600	98	25,5
Zimbabwe	3,1	1,8	4,5	117	52	5	7 100	79	256,1
Zambia	2,7	1,7	3,7	97[1]	20[1]	2[1]	10 900	88	334,7
Botswana	2,5	2,5	2,6	119	54	3	5 150	50	104,7
Kenya	2,3	1,3	3,1	95	29	2	10 150	95	115,5
Madagascar	2,2	1,7	2,6	92	19	3	8 100	82	0,1
Tanzania	2,0	1,3	2,8	69	5	..	25 000	92	134,5
Malawi	1,7	1,1	2,4	66	4	1	45 750	96	297,9
Namibia	1,7	..	..	119	41	3	4 600	92	322,0
Mozambique	1,6	1,2	2,2	63	8	0,3	50 000	66	5,4
Zaire	1,6	0,8	2,4	87[2]	28[2]	1,5[2]	..	43	55,3
Angola	1,5	1,0	2,0	91	12	1	14 300	53	6,8

[1]1988; [2]1985

Sources: Africa Institute, World Bank

5.1 Human Development Index for developing countries (1993)

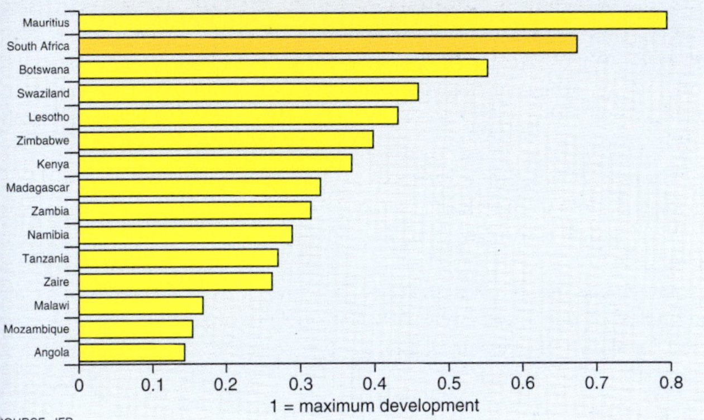

SOURCE: IFR

5.2 Growth in GNP per capita (1985 – 93)

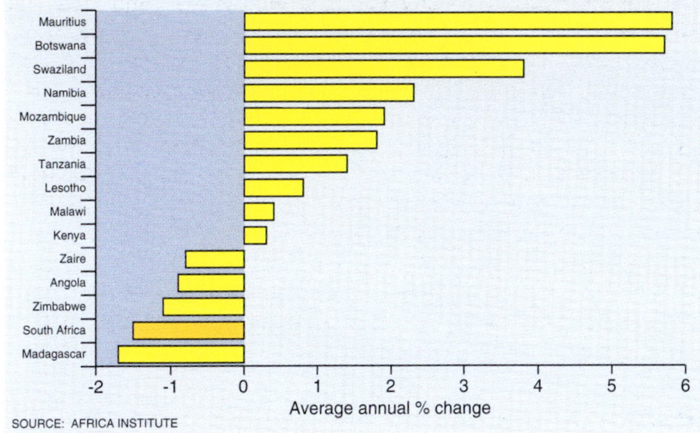

SOURCE: AFRICA INSTITUTE

5.3 Pupils per teacher (primary level, 1991 – 92)

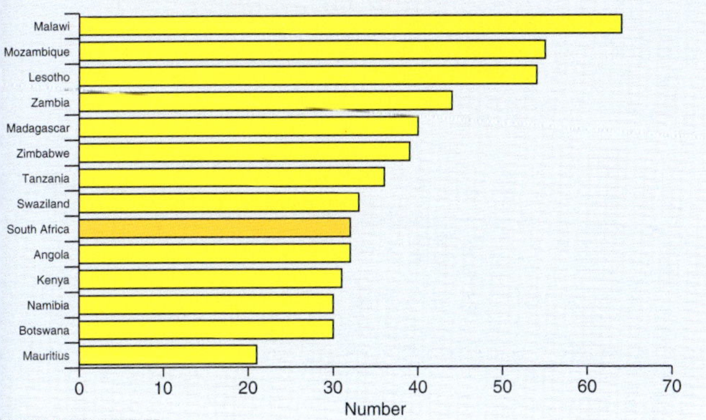

SOURCE: AFRICA INSTITUTE

5.4 Tertiary students (1988 – 92)

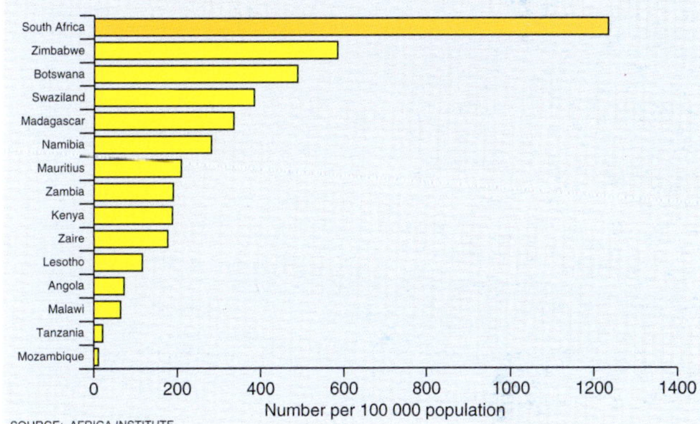

SOURCE: AFRICA INSTITUTE

5.5 Level of nutrition (average daily calorie intake, 1992)

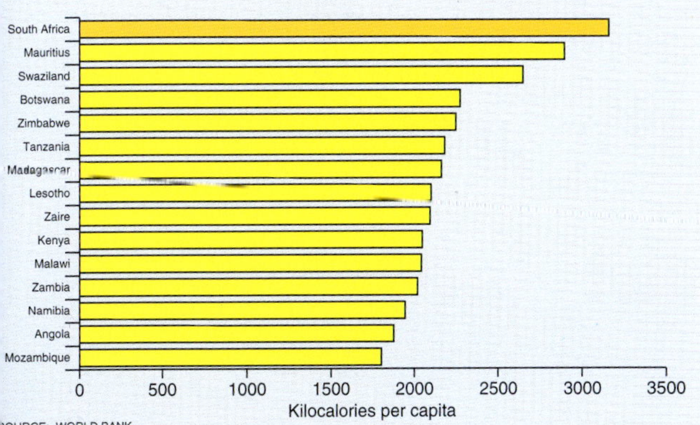

SOURCE: WORLD BANK

5.6 Cumulative AIDS cases reported* (early 1980s until 1993/94)

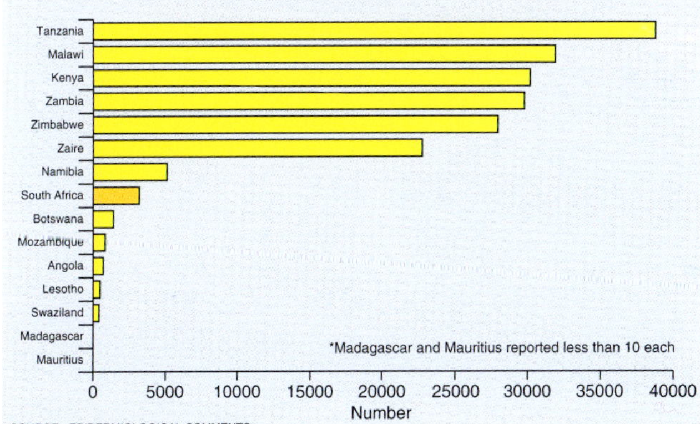

SOURCE: EPIDERMIOLOGICAL COMMENTS

6 Economic infrastructure

A country's economic infrastructure is the backbone of its industrial development and incorporates all man-made structures (transport, water, electricity and communication systems) which facilitate economic activity.

For every 1 000 km² of land, Africa has 53 km of road, of which 12 km is paved. Africa also has 2,8 km of rail track per 1 000 km². South Africa has 149 km of road, 43 km of paved road and 19,3 km of rail track per 1 000 km².

The Kariba Dam, in the Zambezi River on the border between Zambia and Zimbabwe, has the largest capacity (185 000 million m³) of all dams in Africa. The Cahora Bassa Dam, also in the Zambezi River but situated in Mozambique, is the second largest, with a capacity of 66 000 million m³. These two dams have electricity generating capacities of 1 350 MW and 2 076 MW respectively. The largest dam in South Africa is the Gariep Dam in the Orange River, with a capacity of 5 670 million m³, followed by Vanderkloof (3 236 million m³), Sterkfontein (2 617 million m³), Vaal (2 529 million m³) and Pongolapoort (2 446 million m³).

The Lesotho Highlands Water Project (LHWP), currently under construction, will divert water from the Orange River via the Vaal-Wilge River system to the Vaal Dam for consumption in the South African Gauteng province early in the next century. The project will be developed in four phases over a period of about 25 years. The total project will consist of six dams with a storage capacity of more than 6 500 million m³, four pump stations, a hydropower station with a generating capacity of 110 MW, and 225 km of tunnels. In the light of the joint development and utilisation of Southern Africa's water resources, the construction of the LHWP is regarded as being of great importance.

In the longer term, ie after the full implementation of the LHWP around the year 2011, further sources of water for the fast growing South African Gauteng province will have to be found. The Zambezi River seems to be the most promising source in this regard. It has a total annual flow of some 100 billion m³, which is about double that of all South Africa's rivers combined.

Mozambique, despite having two important ports of its own (Maputo and Beira), shipped almost 18 000 t of exports through South Africa's Durban harbour in 1993. During 1993 South Africa's ports also handled nearly 78 000 t of exports and imports for Botswana, 33 420 t for Lesotho, 46 000 t for Swaziland, 227 000 t for Zambia, and 813 500 t for Zimbabwe. An average of 110 South African rail wagons cross the border daily into Mozambique, 213 into Botswana and 1 482 into Zimbabwe, Zambia and Zaire. Had it not been for South African railways and harbours, there would have been severe logistical difficulties in bringing famine relief to much of Southern Africa when drought devastated maize crops in 1991-92.

TABLE 6.1: INFRASTRUCTURE INDICATORS (1990-94)

	Electricity			Transport						Communication
	Net generating capacity (MW)			Railways	Paved roads		Air transport		Harbours	Telephones
	Total	Thermal	Hydro	km	km	% of total road network	Passengers passenger-km million	Freight ton-km million	Tonnage handled '000 t	Mainline connections '000
South Africa	**39 905[1]**	**35 945**	**2 120**	**21 245**	**58 000**	**31**	**8 413**	**191**	**111 500**	**5 200**
Zaire	2 584	51	2 533	4 000	2 800	2	384	33	4 000	40
Zimbabwe	1 966	1 300	666	2 745	15 800	19	817	64	landlocked	300
Zambia	1 633	–	1 633	2 190	6 500	18	655	22	landlocked	92
Kenya	655[2]	37	586	2 040	7 000	11	1 479	39	7 000	383
Angola	523	199	324	2 900	8 600	12	1 241	42	22 500	75
Namibia	360	120	240	2 380	4 100	8	423	2	700	92
Tanzania	351	–	351	3 570	3 600	4	284	4	7 000	140
Mauritius	313	253	60	–	1 700	91	2 464	81	3 000	75
Mozambique	252	157	95[3]	3 150	4 600	17	465	9	6 000	66
Madagascar	220	114	106	1 020	4 700	12	387	26	1 500	37
Malawi	190	25	165	780	2 400	18	87	1	landlocked	50
Botswana	174	174	–	1 100	1 600	14	73	–	landlocked	48
Swaziland	51	10	41	370	510	18	45	–	landlocked	25
Lesotho	5	2	3	2	570	8	14	–	landlocked	19

[1] Inclucing nuclear (1 840 MW)
[2] Including geothermal (31 MW)
[3] Excluding Cahora Bassa

Sources: Africa Institute, Eskom

6.1 Electricity grid

6.2 Main roads network

6.3 Railways and ports

6.4 Pipelines and gasfields

7 Economic growth and development

The number of countries in sub-Saharan Africa with IMF-sponsored Structural Adjustment Programmes (SAPs) have increased from almost none in the early 1980s to 24 in the early 1990s. According to the IMF, countries that have successfully implemented SAPs have significantly reduced their domestic and external imbalances. Together with this, real GDP growth has increased, while real GDP per capita has also improved in these countries.

South Africa as the major economic power within Southern Africa constitutes about 70% of the region's total GNP and produces around 84% of its electricity. The country is also prominent regarding agricultural production, as is evident from table 7.2. Despite this, South Africa's economic performance has been quite poor in comparison with the other countries in the region since the mid-1980s (see graph 7.4B), emphasising the impact that inter alia trade and financial sanctions had on the South African economy during this period.

Regarding the composition of GDP in the Southern African region, graph 7.2 shows that agriculture is still an important economic activity. In 8 countries the agricultural sector contributed more than 15% of GDP in 1992, while in 12 of the 15 countries it was more than 10% of GDP in that year. The composition of South Africa's GDP in 1994 was as follows: agriculture accounted for 4,7%, mining for 8,7%, manufacturing for 23,5% and the services sector for 55,9%.

TABLE 7.1: INDICATORS OF ECONOMIC GROWTH AND DEVELOPMENT

	Total GNP $ million		Real value added by sector average annual % change, 1986-93			Electricity production GWh 1991	Classification of economies by income[8] 1995
	1983	1993	Agriculture	Industry[1]	Services		
South Africa	**73 160**	**118 057**	**0,0**	**0,1**	**1,4**	**155 812**	**upper-middle-income**
Kenya	6 450	6 743	2,0	3,9	4,5	3 600	low-income
Zimbabwe	5 820	5 756	-2,6[3]	2,7[5]	3,8[5]	7 468	low-income
Zaire	5 050	8 120[4]	2,5[6]	-0,5[6]	2,0[6]	5 581	low-income
Tanzania	4 880	2 521	4,9[5]	6,3[5]	2,7[5]	1 879	low-income
Zambia	3 630	3 152	-0,2	2,5	-0,1	6 461	low-income
Angola	3 320[2]	5 996[3]	0,5[7]	6,4[7]	1,8[7]	935	lower-middle-income
Mozambique	2 810[2]	1 375	0,6	7,4	8,7	284	low-income
Madagascar	2 730	3 039	2,5	1,2	1,2	569	low-income
Namibia	1 531	2 594	3,9[5]	-0,4[5]	4,3[5]	1 003	lower-middle-income
Malawi	1 390	2 034	1,8	4,7	3,4	782	low-income
Mauritius	1 250	3 309	0,0	8,4	6,3	813	upper-middle-income
Botswana	920	3 630	9,3	5,2	13,3	1 015	lower-middle-income
Lesotho	670	1 254	-2,4	14,1	4,7	1	low-income
Swaziland	610	933	-2,1	12,2	3,2	84	lower-middle-income

[1]Including mining
[2]1980; [3]1989; [4]1990; [5]1986-92; [6]1986-89; [7]1986-90
[8]Classification according to 1993 GNP per capita in US$. The groups are: low-income, $695 or less; lower-middle-income, $696-$2 785; and upper-middle-income, $2 786-$8 625
Sources: Africa Institute, Eskom, World Bank

TABLE 7.2: AGRICULTURAL AND FORESTRY PRODUCTION

	Area permanently under crops '000 ha 1991	Sugar cane '000 t 1992	Cotton lint '000 t 1992	Ground-nuts '000 t 1992	Maize '000 t 1993	Fresh fruit '000 t 1992	Fresh cows' milk '000 t 1992	Red & white meat '000 t 1992	Fish catch '000 t 1990	Roundwood production '000 m³ 1992
South Africa	**13 174**	**18 500**	**22**	**116**	**9 425**	**3 890**	**2 390**	**1 392**	**536**	**41 712**
Zaire	7 880	1 150	26	440	930	3 088	7	212	162	43 243
Zambia	5 268	1 150	10	21	1 598	97	84	105	65	13 790
Angola	3 450	–	–	–	274	–	–	–	–	–
Tanzania	3 370	1 410	73	65	2 282	2 133	460	285	377	34 903
Mozambique	3 130	–	–	–	533	306	68	71	35	–
Madagascar	3 102	1 900	10	34	145[2]	753	475	285	107	8 597
Zimbabwe	2 814	3 236	27	107[2]	2 562	140	415	130	25	8 033
Kenya	2 440	4 430	9	14	1 748	969	1 810	352	142	37 311
Malawi	1 690	1 950	5	23	2 034	432	40	40	80	9 706
Botswana	1 400	–	–	–	7	–	–	–	–	–
Namibia	662	–	–	–	32	–	70	93	290	–
Lesotho	340	–	–	–	92	–	–	–	–	–
Swaziland	209	3 600	10	3	84	–	–	–	–	2 297
Mauritius	106	6 400	–	2	4[1]	10[1]	25[1]	10[1]	–	12

[1]1989; [2]1991
Sources: Africa Institute, World Bank

7.1 Areas of economic development

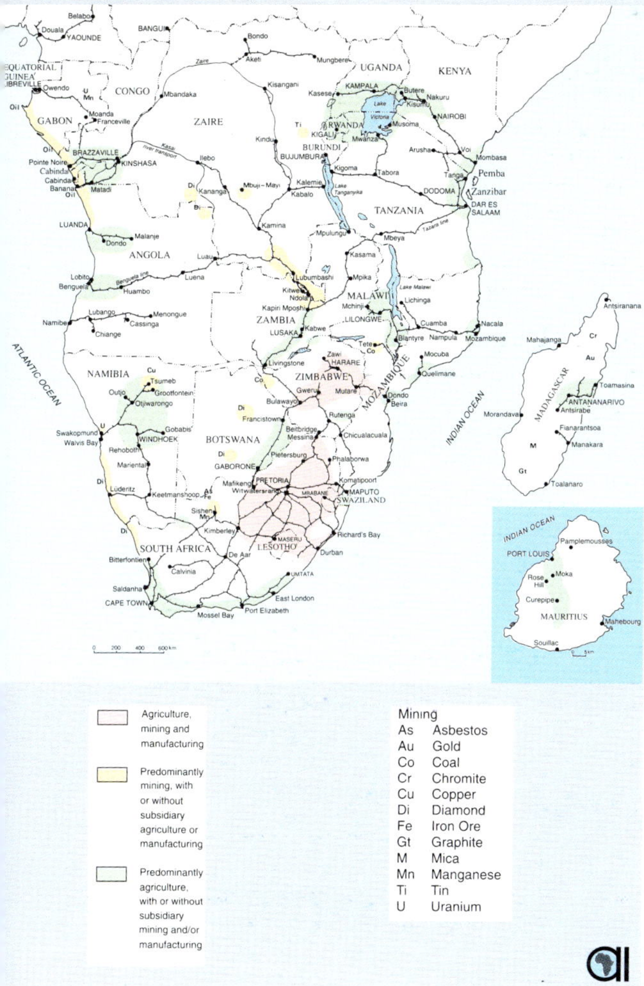

7.2 Composition of GDP
(%, 1992)

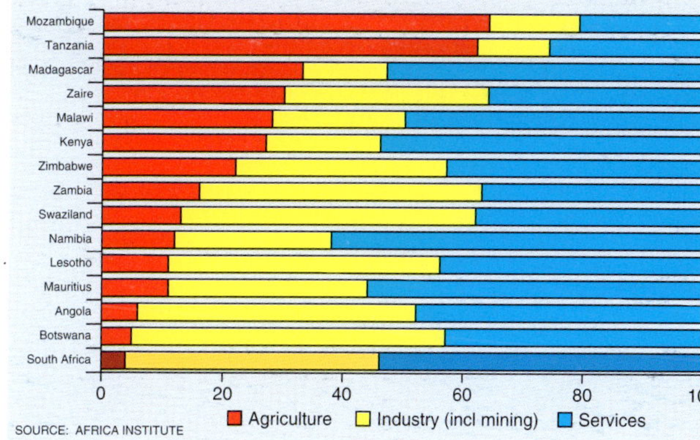

SOURCE: AFRICA INSTITUTE

7.3 Manufacturing as % of GDP
(1992)

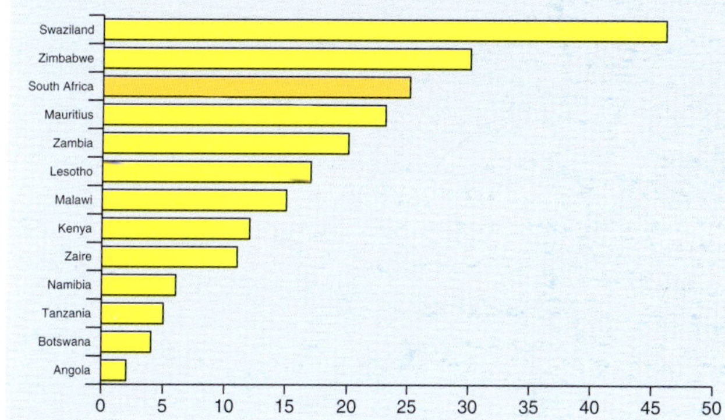

SOURCE: AFRICA INSTITUTE

7.4 Real GDP growth

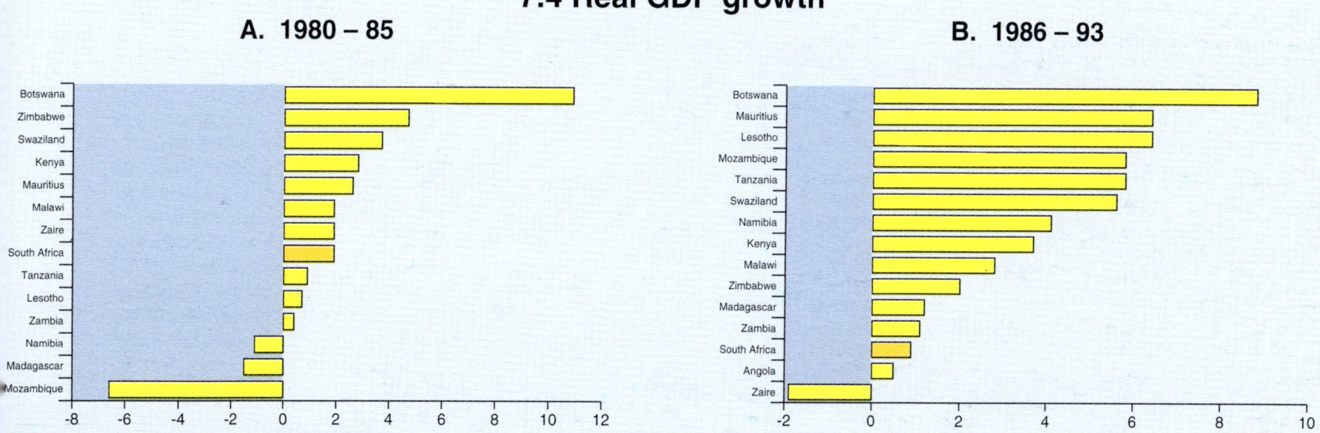

SOURCE: WORLD BANK

8 Consumption and saving

The propensity to consume is relatively high in the countries in Southern Africa (see graph 8.1), but not completely out of line with, for example, the G7 industrial countries (USA, Japan, Germany, France, Italy, United Kingdom and Canada). Total consumption expenditure (private plus government consumption) as a percentage of GDP was on average about 76% in the G7 industrial countries during the early 1990s. As shown in table 8.1, private consumption expenditure, however, constitutes the larger portion of total consumption expenditure in the Southern African economies, with South Africa no exception.

Government consumption expenditure as a percentage of GDP declined on an annual average basis between the periods 1980-85 and 1986-93 in the following Southern African countries: Botswana, Kenya, Lesotho, Madagascar, Malawi, Mauritius, Mozambique, Swaziland, Tanzania, and Zambia. However, in Namibia, South Africa, Zaire and Zimbabwe this ratio increased.

Gross domestic saving as a percentage of GDP was extremely low in certain countries in the region during 1993 (see table 8.1). In two countries, namely Lesotho and Mozambique, it was negative by quite a large percentage. In South Africa, the general government has dissaved continuously since 1984. As a result, net domestic saving (the total of private, corporate and government saving, but excluding depreciation) as a percentage of GDP has declined significantly from 13% per annum during the 1980s to only 3,5% per annum during 1990-94.

TABLE 8.1: CONSUMPTION AND SAVING INDICATORS

	Year	Private consumption		Government consumption		Gross domestic saving % of GDP
		% of GDP	% of total consumption	% of GDP	% of total consumption	
Lesotho	1993	111,7	82,4	30,4	17,6	-42,1
Mozambique	1993	94,2	84,9	16,8	15,1	-11,0
Madagascar	1993	91,5	93,3	6,6	6,7	1,9
Tanzania	1992	84,9	89,0	10,5	11,0	4,6
Zambia	1993	81,4	89,9	9,1	10,1	9,5
Malawi	1993	78,0	82,2	16,9	17,8	5,1
Swaziland	1993	73,1	74,3	25,3	25,7	1,6
Zaire	1992	68,8	76,0	21,7	24,0	9,5
Kenya	1993	65,8	83,4	13,1	16,6	21,1
Namibia	1992	65,4	66,4	33,1	33,6	1,5
Mauritius	1993	65,0	85,8	10,8	14,2	24,2
Zimbabwe	1993	59,9	76,1	18,8	23,9	21,3
South Africa	**1993**	**59,5**	**73,8**	**21,1**	**26,2**	**19,4**
Angola	1990	44,7	61,1	28,5	38,9	26,8
Botswana	1993	40,4	62,2	24,6	37,8	35,0

Sources: IMF, World Bank

8.1 Total consumption
(annual average, 1986 – 93)

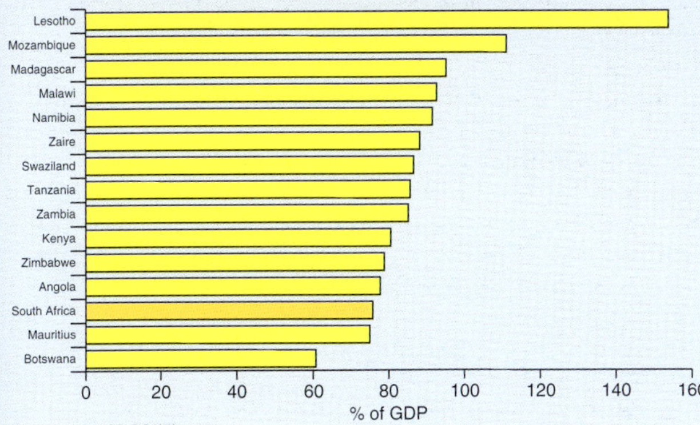

SOURCES: IMF, WORLD BANK

8.2 Real private consumption per capita
(1989 – 92)

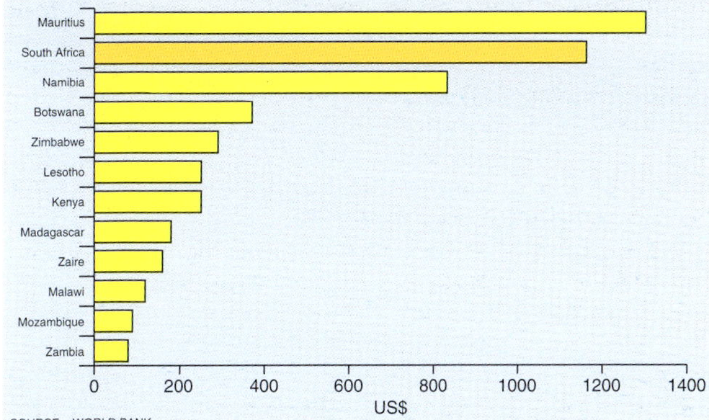

SOURCE: WORLD BANK

8.3 Real private consumption
(1980 – 92)

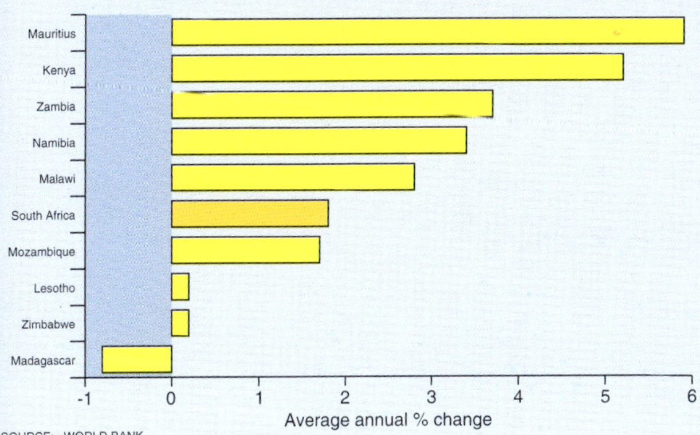

SOURCE: WORLD BANK

8.4 Real government consumption
(1980 – 92)

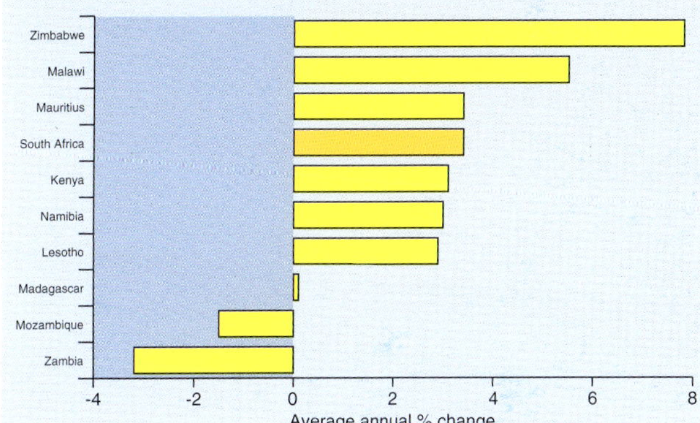

SOURCE: WORLD BANK

8.5 Private consumption
(1992/93)

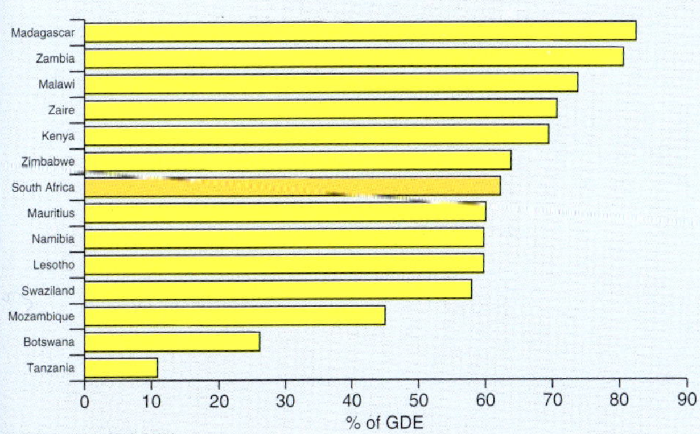

SOURCES: IMF, WORLD BANK

8.6 Government consumption
(1992/93)

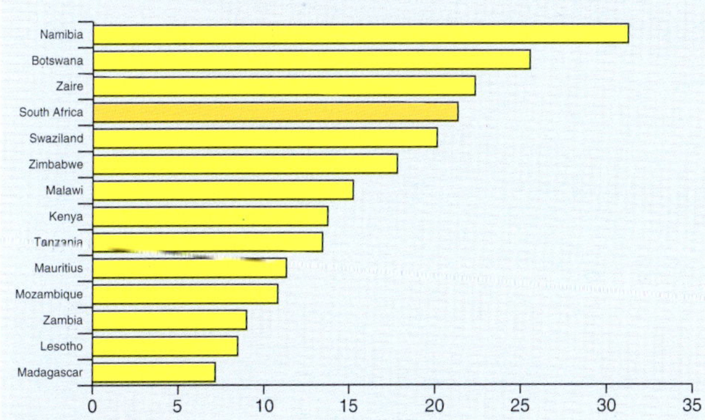

SOURCES: IMF, WORLD BANK

9 Investment

The generally accepted international standard for gross domestic fixed investment for developing countries is about 25% of GDP. In the Southern African region only 5 of the 15 countries meet this standard (see table 9.1). Lesotho's relatively high ratio of gross domestic fixed investment to GDP (78,7%) can be ascribed to the construction of the Lesotho Highlands Water Project (LHWP), which commenced in the late 1980s.

South Africa's gross domestic fixed investment/GDP ratio was on an upward trend during the 1960s and 1970s as transport, electricity, water and communication networks were put into place. In the industrial sector, petro-chemical (Sasol) and iron and steel (Iscor) plants were erected which also contributed to strong growth in fixed investment during those years. However, there have been no major capital investment projects (except Mossgas to the amount of approximately R11 billion in 1989) since the beginning of the 1980s. This resulted in a steady decline in the fixed investment/GDP ratio from an unsurpassed high of 30,1% in 1976 to a record low of only 15,4% in 1993, after which there has been some improvement again. Some other reasons for the deterioration in South Africa's investment trend may be

- the impact of trade and financial sanctions during the eighties and early nineties;
- high real interest rates at times;
- a depreciating exchange rate;
- declining investment by the government sector; and
- political uncertainty.

The Industrial Development Corporation (IDC) has estimated that total investment spending on main capital projects in South Africa will amount to R107,4 billion during the period 1995-2005. Of this amount, 20,4% will be spent in the mining industry, 42,2% on manufacturing and agriculture-based projects, 30% on infrastructure (electricity, water and transport) and 7,4% on property development projects. Increased social spending via the government's Reconstruction and Development Programme may also increase the ratio of gross domestic fixed investment to GDP in coming years.

TABLE 9.1: INVESTMENT INDICATORS

	Year	Gross domestic investment (GDI)			Gross domestic fixed investment		
		% of GDP	% of GDE	Real GDI per capita US$, 1992	% of GDP	% of GDE	% of GDI
Lesotho	1992	78,3	36,0	240	78,7	36,2	100,5
Mozambique	1993	68,8	44,2	30	68,8	44,2	100,0
Tanzania	1993	63,6	75,7	40	57,6	68,7	90,7
Botswana	1989	41,8	48,4	1 060[1]	40,8	47,2	97,6
Mauritius	1993	30,6	28,7	620	28,8	27,1	94,4
Zimbabwe	1992	20,5	18,5	180	18,2	18,8	92,0
Swaziland	1992	19,2	22,0	120	19,2	22,0	100,0
Kenya	1993	16,0	16,9	60	15,3	16,1	95,7
South Africa	**1993**	**16,0**	**16,5**	**340**	**15,4**	**15,9**	**96,1**
Malawi	1993	12,3	11,1	30	10,0	9,1	81,7
Angola	1990	11,7	..	..	..	..	..
Madagascar	1993	11,4	10,4	20	11,4	10,4	100,0
Zambia	1993	10,7	10,6	90[2]	6,5	6,4	60,5
Namibia	1993	9,6	9,1	130	10,6	10,0	110,2
Zaire	1992	6,9	7,1	30[1]	7,1	7,3	103,0

[1]1989; [2]1991

Sources: IMF, World Bank

9.1 Investment and economic growth (1980 – 92)

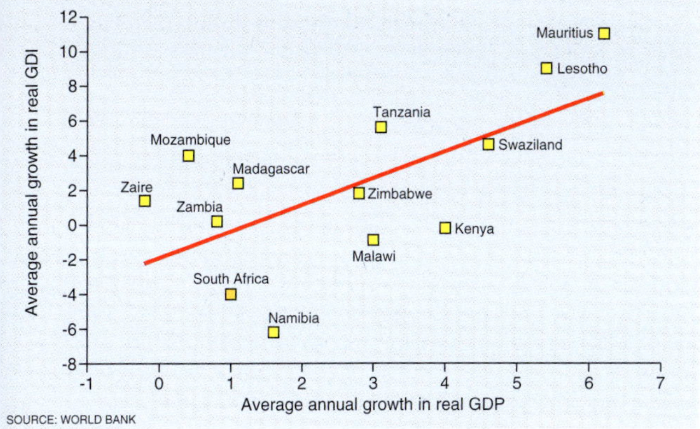

SOURCE: WORLD BANK

9.2 Foreign direct investment (1993)

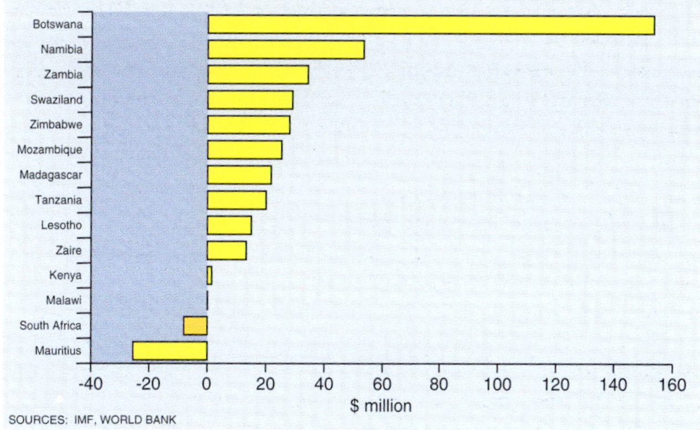

SOURCES: IMF, WORLD BANK

9.3 Real gross domestic investment (1980 – 92)

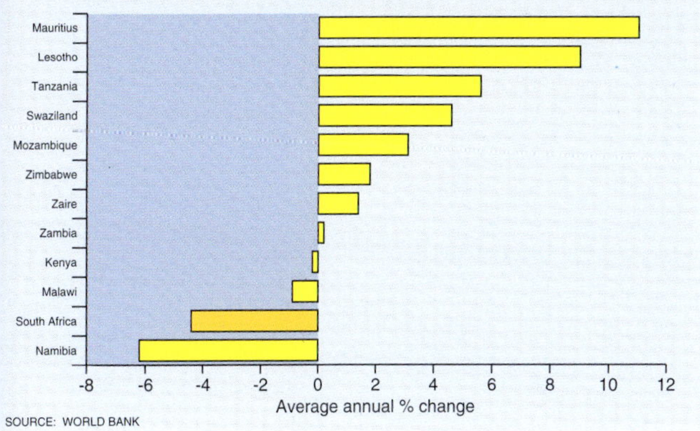

SOURCE: WORLD BANK

9.4 Real gross domestic fixed investment (1980 – 92)

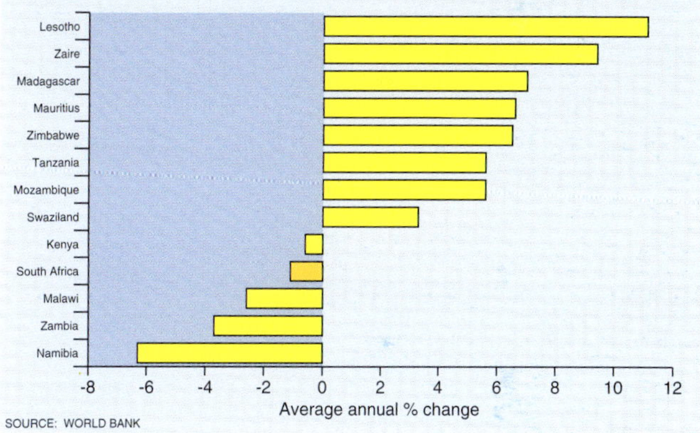

SOURCE: WORLD BANK

9.5 Gross public sector investment (annual average, 1986 – 92/93)

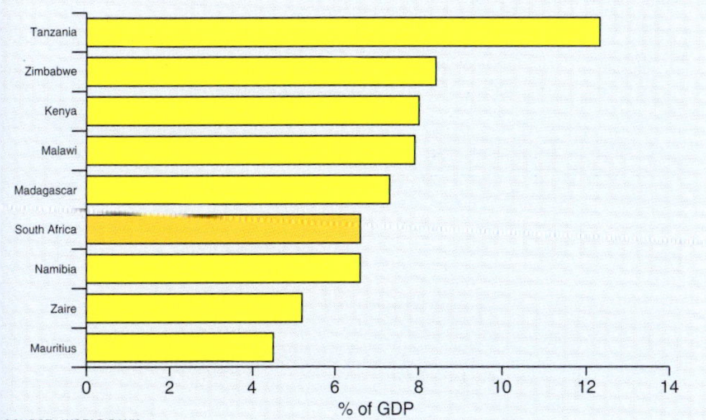

SOURCE: WORLD BANK

9.6 Gross private sector investment (annual average, 1986 – 92/93)

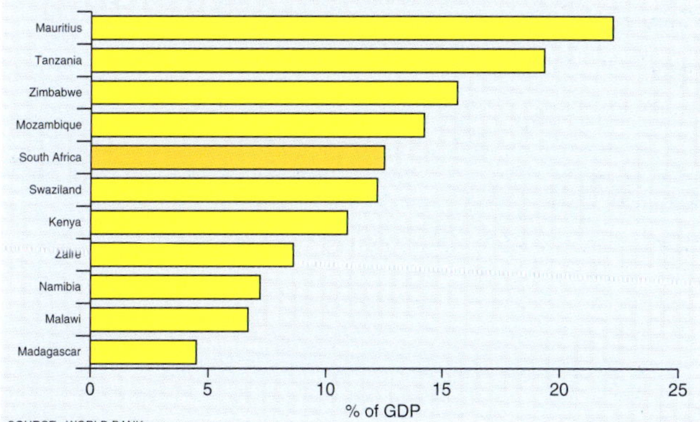

SOURCE: WORLD BANK

10 Labour market

The total number of new entrants to the labour market in the SADC countries (excluding Tanzania) increased from 249 000 per annum during 1970-75 to 366 000 per annum during 1985-90. The total number of new employment opportunities created in the formal sector in these countries, however, declined from 156 000 per annum during 1970-75 to only 33 000 per annum during 1985-90. As a result of these contrasting labour force and employment trends, the absorption rate of the total labour market declined from 63% per annum during 1970-75 to just 9% per annum during 1985-90. Since 1990 this situation has deteriorated even further.

The total labour force in Southern Africa was about 86 million people in 1992 (42% of the total population). South Africa's labour force comprised 16,3 million people in 1992, ie 41% of the country's population and 19% of the region's total labour force.

The expected increase in labour force growth in Southern Africa in years to come (see graph 10.3) is related to high population growth projections (see graph 4.1) and the fact that more than 40% of the population in 13 of the 15 countries in the region are 14 years of age or younger (see graph 4.3).

The fact that agriculture is an important economic activity in most Southern African countries (see graph 7.2) is confirmed by the sectoral composition of the labour force in these countries (see graph 10.2A). In 9 of the 15 countries the agricultural sector accounts for more than 70% of the total labour force.

TABLE 10.1: LABOUR MARKET INDICATORS FOR SELECTED COUNTRIES (MANUFACTURING SECTOR, 1987 = 100)

	Year	Employment	Real earnings/employee	Real output/employee	Earnings as % of value added
Botswana	1988	165,3	102,3	133,8	34,9
Swaziland	1988	107,6	102,1	115,5	23,0
Tanzania	1988	101,7	87,9	104,9	24,9
Madagascar	1988	100,9	87,4	92,2	37,3
Zimbabwe	1990	111,5	111,8	102,5	34,2
Kenya	1990	109,6	91,2	124,5	42,2
Mauritius	1990	107,2	109,3	120,5	45,5
South Africa	**1990**	**102,2**	**105,9**	**97,7**	**48,7**
Zambia	1990	101,1	59,4	76,7	26,8

Source: World Bank

TABLE 10.2: EARNINGS PER EMPLOYEE FOR SELECTED COUNTRIES AND SECTORS (AVERAGE MONTHLY FIGURES IN CURRENT US$)

	Mining and quarrying		Manufacturing		Construction		Transport, storage and communication	
	1983	Most recent	1983	Most recent	1983	Most recent	1983	Most recent
Swaziland	577	309[1]	724	397[1]	391	192[1]	328	192[1]
South Africa	**381**	**514[3]**	**567**	**675[3]**	**431**	**448[3]**	**595**	**826[3]**
Botswana	277	374[4]	153	215[4]	147	184[4]	202	445[4]
Zimbabwe	254	179[4]	337	206[4]	258	97[4]	464	292[4]
Mauritius	177	302[4]	135	255[4]	154	364[4]	205	380[4]
Kenya	135	93[3]	126	121[3]	99	95[3]	178	171[3]
Malawi	33	17[1]	68	65[2]	40	30[2]	67	63[2]

[1]1989; [2]1990; [3]1991; [4]1992
Source: World Bank

TABLE 10.3: EMPLOYEES ON SOUTH AFRICAN MINES[1] (AVERAGE NUMBER BY COUNTRY OF ORIGIN)

	Total		Gold Mines		Coal mines		Other mines	
	1983	1993	1983	1993	1983	1993	1983	1993
South Africa	**311 624**	**211 778**	**245 718**	**157 996**	**43 842**	**17 911**	**22 064**	**35 871**
Lesotho	109 470	88 203	96 409	79 530	9 730	3 186	3 331	5 487
Mozambique	45 836	49 703	42 473	41 553	1 321	1 100	2 042	7 050
Botswana	18 679	12 930	17 225	10 681	60	1	1 394	2 248
Malawi	16 376	–	14 287	–	227	–	1 862	–
Swaziland	11 513	15 894	10 624	14 471	679	316	210	1 107
Zimbabwe	8	2	1	1	7	1	–	–
Other countries	1 269	712	1 266	545	–	13	3	154
Total	514 775	379 222	428 003	304 777	55 866	22 528	30 906	51 917
Total excluding South Africa	203 151	167 444	182 285	146 781	12 024	4 617	8 842	16 046
Foreign workers as % of total	39,5	44,2	42,6	48,2	21,5	20,5	28,6	30,9

[1]Member mines of the Chamber of Mines of South Africa
Source: Chamber of Mines of South Africa

10.1 Size of labour force (1992)

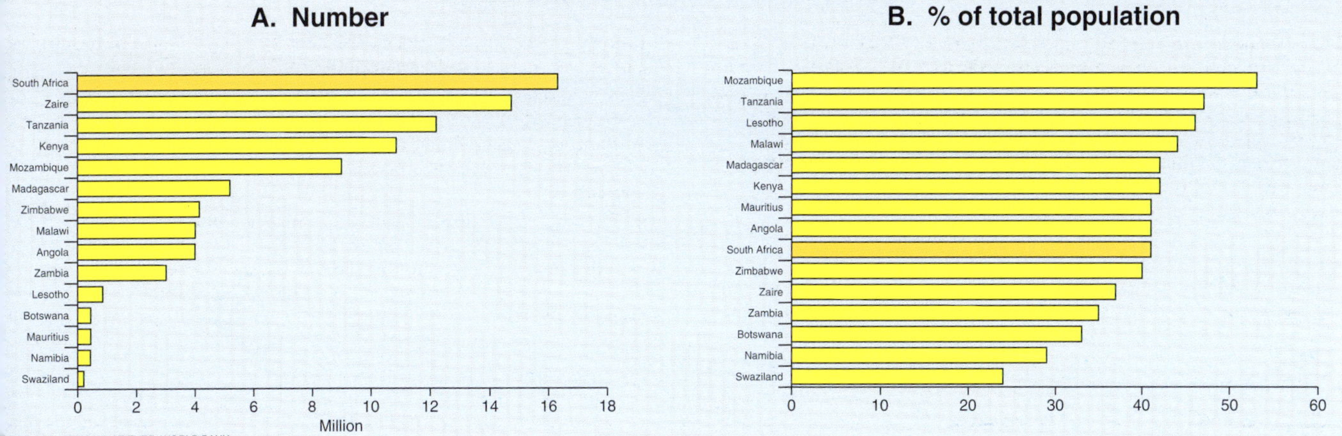

SOURCES: AFRICA INSTITUTE, WORLD BANK

10.2 Composition of labour force (%, 1992)

SOURCE: AFRICA INSTITUTE

10.3 Labour force growth

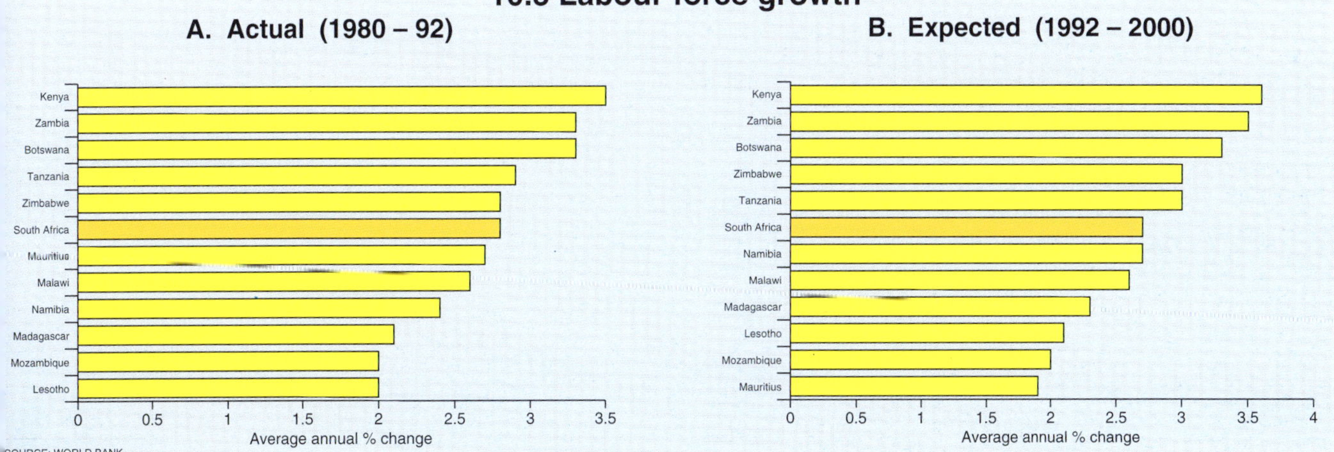

SOURCE: WORLD BANK

11 Government finance

Government debt in 1991 as a percentage of GDP varied substantially between the countries in Southern Africa. Botswana had the lowest debt to GDP ratio (12,7%), while Zaire had the highest (120,3%). Zaire's government debt to GDP ratio was even higher in 1992 (128,8%). For some other countries in the region this ratio was as follows in 1991: 40,3% for South Africa, 44,3% for Mauritius, 70% for Lesotho and 73,6% for Zimbabwe in 1990. South Africa's government debt to GDP ratio, however, increased sharply to a record high of 55,4% in 1994.

Interest payments on government debt as a percentage of GDP varied from as low as 0,7% for Botswana to as high as 5,6% for Kenya in 1993. The corresponding figure for Zimbabwe was 5,1%, followed by South Africa with 4,7%, Mozambique with 3,6%, Malawi with 2,7%, Zambia with 2,5%, Mauritius with 2,1%, Madagascar with 2,0% and Namibia and Swaziland with 0,8% each.

Of all the countries in the region, South Africa in 1991 had the highest tax revenue from income and profits, ie direct taxes (see table 11.1). The biggest source of direct tax revenue in South Africa is individual tax (37,8% of total tax revenue in 1994), while corporate tax was only 12,1% of total taxes in 1994. Indirect taxes were 49,9% of total tax revenue in 1994, compared to 45,7% in 1984 and 34,5% in 1974.

Regarding capital expenditure by the government, South Africa spent proportionately the least of all the countries in the region in 1991, while in Mozambique the government spent proportionately the most (see table 11.2). The Lesotho government's capital expenditure ratio of 35,9% in 1991 (the second highest in the region) may be related to the construction of the Lesotho Highlands Water Project.

TABLE 11.1: MAJOR COMPONENTS OF GOVERNMENT REVENUE (% OF TOTAL REVENUE, 1991)

	Tax revenue								Non-tax revenue
	Total	Income, profits and capital gains where applicable			Goods and services		International trade and transactions	Other tax revenue	
		Total	Individual	Corporate	Total	Sales tax/VAT			
Mauritius	94,1	13,7	5,4	8,3	22,7	8,4	46,7	11,0	5,9
South Africa	**93,8**	**52,6**	**36,3**	**15,9**	**33,2**	**22,7**	**3,8**	**4,2**	**6,2**
Zambia[1]	91,4	38,1	7,8	27,8	37,0	23,5	15,8	0,5	8,6
Zimbabwe	90,6	44,4	26,9	16,1	26,3	18,4	18,9	1,0	9,4
Kenya	89,2	26,1	..	..	47,9	37,2	14,2	1,0	10,8
Zaire	88,9	29,9	25,4	4,4	15,2	4,1	30,8	13,0	11,1
Tanzania	88,7	..	..	..	..	..	16,5	..	11,3
Swaziland[2]	88,4	38,6	10,2	26,6	12,9	12,2	36,2	0,7	11,6
Malawi[3]	86,9	36,9	12,1	24,5	33,0	29,0	16,3	0,7	13,1
Namibia	86,6	22,2	16,9	5,3	22,7	15,2	40,9	0,8	13,4
Lesotho	85,5	16,9	9,2	7,7	16,7	13,7	51,8	0,1	14,5
Mozambique	85,0	..	..	..	..	..	..	..	15,0
Angola	81,0	20,5	..	..	..	..	1,0	..	19,0
Madagascar	78,3	14,9	5,0	8,2	19,0	6,6	43,3	1,1	21,7
Botswana	51,3	30,0	3,1	24,0	2,0	1,8	19,2	0,1	48,7

[1]1988; [2]1989; [3]1990
Sources: IMF, World Bank

TABLE 11.2: MAJOR COMPONENTS OF GOVERNMENT EXPENDITURE (% OF TOTAL EXPENDITURE, 1991)

	Current expenditure						Capital expenditure
	Total	Expenditure on goods and services			Interest payments	Subsidies and transfers	
		Total	Wages and salaries	Other goods and services			
South Africa	**93,3**	**54,4**	**24,0**	**30,4**	**14,7**	**24,2**	**6,7**
Angola	89,8	70,2	53,0	17,2	14,6	5,0	10,2
Tanzania	89,5	60,5	24,8	35,7	13,2	15,8	10,5
Zimbabwe	88,9	55,1	38,0	17,1	15,6	18,2	11,1
Zaire	87,5	80,2	35,0	45,2	2,0	5,3	12,5
Namibia	85,3	73,2	45,0	28,2	0,8	11,3	14,7
Mauritius	82,7	44,0	34,4	9,6	15,7	23,0	17,3
Kenya	82,5	50,0	29,8	20,2	23,4	9,1	17,5
Botswana	82,5	52,6	27,5	25,1	2,3	27,6	17,5
Zambia	77,8	45,6	21,1	24,5	4,1	28,1	22,2
Swaziland[2]	76,9	58,8	38,6	20,2	5,7	12,4	23,1
Malawi[1]	74,1	52,8	16,9	35,9	16,0	5,3	25,9
Madagascar	64,8	41,9	28,9	13,0	13,4	9,5	35,2
Lesotho	64,1	48,7	29,0	19,7	8,7	6,7	35,9
Mozambique	47,8	37,7	11,6	26,1	4,8	5,3	52,2

[1]1988; [2]1989
Sources: IMF, World Bank

11.1 Government revenue (excluding grants, 1993)

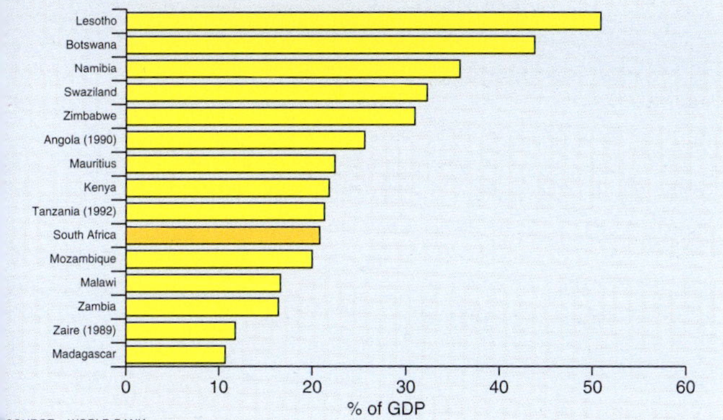

SOURCE: WORLD BANK

11.2 Government expenditure (1993)

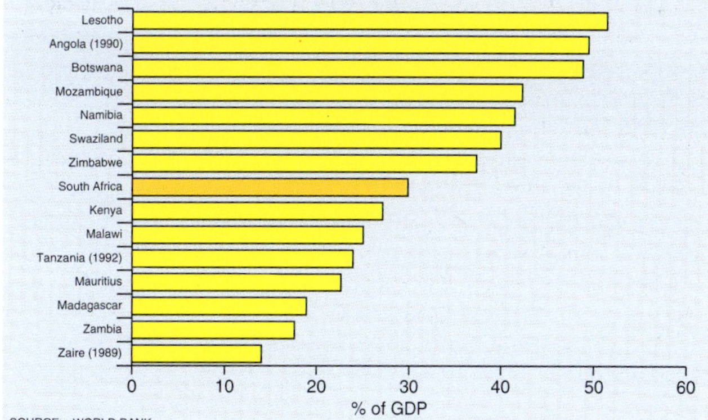

SOURCE: WORLD BANK

11.3 Government deficit/surplus (excluding grants, 1993)

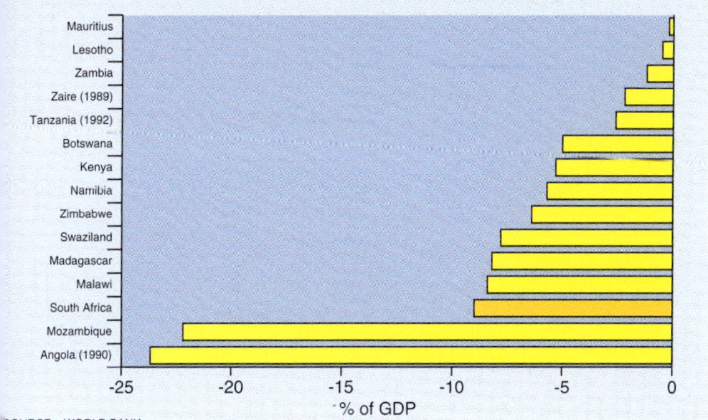

SOURCE: WORLD BANK

11.4 Government expenditure on defence (1990 – 91)

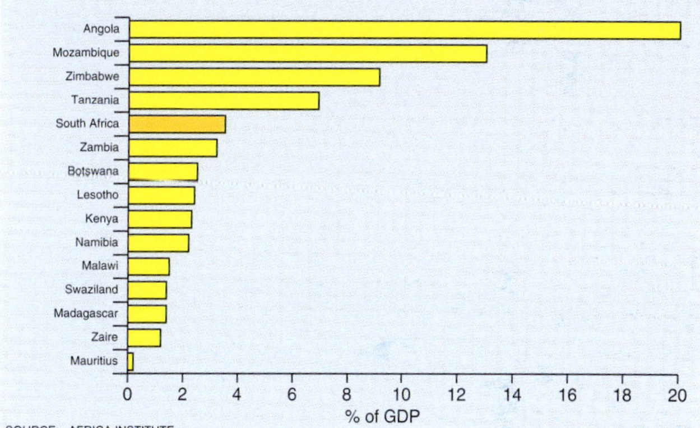

SOURCE: AFRICA INSTITUTE

11.5 Government expenditure on education (1990)

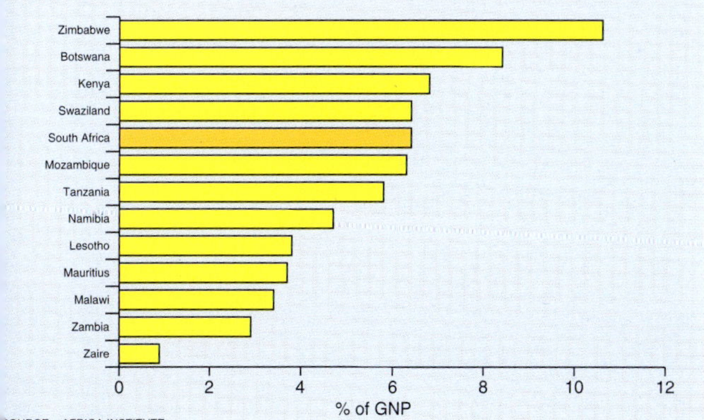

SOURCE: AFRICA INSTITUTE

11.6 Government expenditure on health care (1990)

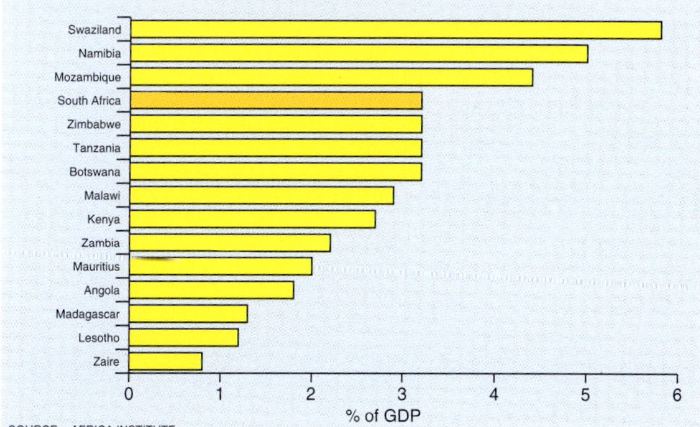

SOURCE: AFRICA INSTITUTE

12 Financial and monetary sector

Until a few years ago, countries in Africa tended to react to balance of payments difficulties and foreign exchange scarcity by tightening exchange controls and trade restrictions. A rapidly growing number of African countries have since realised, however, that the imposition of these restrictions undermines economic growth and financial stability. Major steps have been taken towards the liberalisation of exchange systems (in which the exchange rate became market-determined) by countries such as Kenya, Madagascar, Malawi, Mozambique, Tanzania, Uganda and Zimbabwe.

South Africa's dual exchange rate system, which consisted of the commercial and financial rand, finally came to an end with the abolition of the financial rand in March 1995. All foreign trade transactions, payments and repayments of foreign loans, direct investments into the country and the in- and outflow of capital are now done via the unitary rand, and are reflected on the balance of payments. The exchange controls still in place are expected to be abolished in the course of the next couple of years.

In *The Banker's* 1994 listing of the 100 largest banks in Africa, 27 were in Southern Africa, and 8 of these were in South Africa. Seven of these 8 South African banks were among the top 10 in Africa. The total assets of the top 100 banks in Africa amounted to $116,8 billion in 1994, with the 8 South African banks in the listing accounting for 76,6%. Africa's total banking sector, compared to that of the world, is very small, even with South Africa included. Only 6 African banks made *The Banker's Top 1000* in 1994. These 6 banks were all South African, accounting for less than 0,5% of the world total.

The South African stock market had a market capitalisation of $245 billion towards the end of 1994, followed by that of Egypt ($3,8 billion), Namibia ($3,5 billion), Nigeria ($2,5 billion), Ghana ($2,0 billion), Zimbabwe ($1,7 billion), Mauritius ($835 million), the Ivory Coast ($426 million), Swaziland ($304 million) and Botswana ($293 million).

TABLE 12.1: CURRENCY ARRANGEMENTS (AS OF 31 DECEMBER 1994)

Currency pegged to				Managed floating		Independently floating	
South African rand Currency and country		Composite basket of currencies Currency and country		Currency and country		Currency and country	
Loti	Lesotho	Pula	Botswana	Kwanza	Angola	Kenyan shilling	Kenya
Namibian dollar	Namibia			Mauritian rupee	Mauritius	Malagasy franc	Madagascar
Lilangeni	Swaziland					Malawian kwacha	Malawi
						Metical	Mozambique
						Rand	**South Africa**
						Tanzanian shilling	Tanzania
						New zaire	Zaire
						Zambian kwacha	Zambia
						Zimbabwean dollar	Zimbabwe

Source: IMF

TABLE 12.2: FINANCIAL AND MONETARY INDICATORS

	Exchange rate				Consumer price inflation		Real interest rates in 1993/94			Banks in top 100 in Africa, 1994	
	National currency	Per US$			Average % 1993/94	Year-end % 1993/94	Discount rate year-end %	Lending rate average %	Deposit rate average %	Number	Total assets $ million
		Average 1990	Average 1993/94	End June 1995							
Angola	Kwanza	30	4 788	2 216 915	1 044,0	..	..	..	..	–	–
Botswana	Pula	1,86	2,68	2,75	10,5	9,8	4,5	0,6	-0,8	–	–
Kenya	K shilling	23	56	55	29,0	6,6	14,9	3,2[4]	-1,9[4]	4	893
Lesotho[1]	Loti	2,59	3,55	3,64	8,3	9,8	3,7	6,0	0,1	1	222
Madagascar	Mg franc	1 494	1 914	3 910	38,9	61,2	-2,3[2]	..	..	2	341
Malawi	M kwacha	2,73	10,20	15,32	19,7	19,1	5,0	8,2	1,7	2	399
Mauritius	M rupee	14,84	17,65	17,44	7,3	6,0	7,8	11,6	3,7	3	2 508
Mozambique	Metical	929	6 017	7 300	42,2	42,6	..	..	..	–	–
Namibia[1]	N dollar	2,59	3,55	3,64	10,8	11,3	..	6,3	-1,6	–	–
South Africa[1]	**Rand**	**2,59**	**3,55**	**3,64**	**9,0**	**10,0**	**3,0**	**4,0**	**2,2**	**8**	**89 496**
Swaziland[1]	Lilangeni	2,59	3,55	3,64	14,3	15,4	-3,4	0,7	-6,3	1	1
Tanzania	T shilling	195	515	585	23,5	25,4	-8,7	6,1	-7,3[3]	–	–
Zaire	New zaire	..	1 600	5 331	23 773,1	9 796,9	-97,5	..	..	1	31
Zambia	Z kwacha	30	670	929	189,0	135,6	-29,9	-26,2	-50,1	2	215
Zimbabwe	Z dollar	2,45	8,25	8,55	22,3	21,1	6,9	6,9	1,5	3	98

[1]Member of the Common Monetary Area (CMA)
[2]1988; [3]1989; [4]1990
Sources: Africa Institute, Financial Times, IMF, The Banker

12.1 Domestic credit (1993/94)

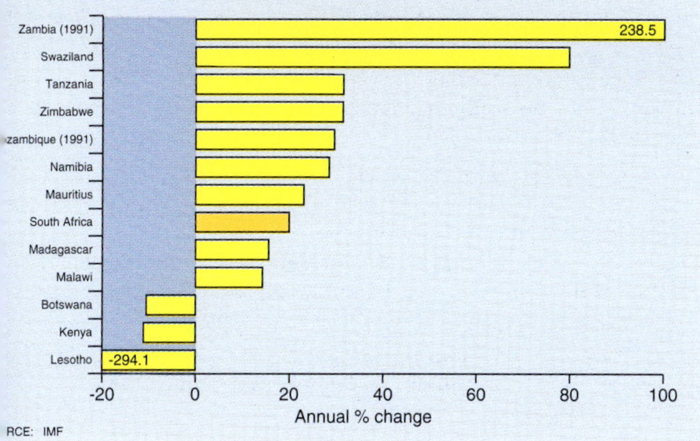

12.2 Private sector credit (1993/94)

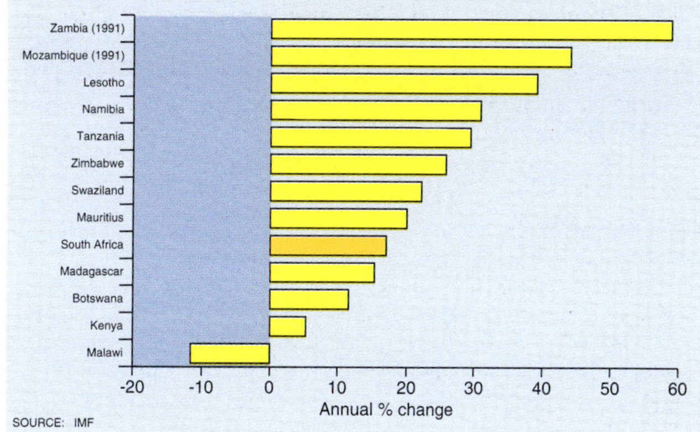

12.3 M1 money supply (1993/94)

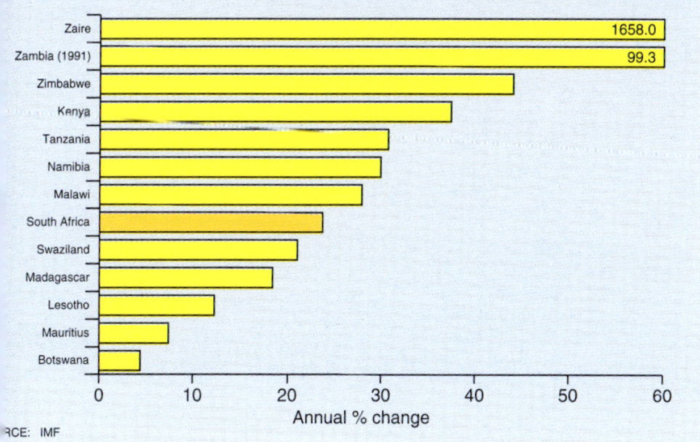

12.4 Real effective exchange rate (1993)

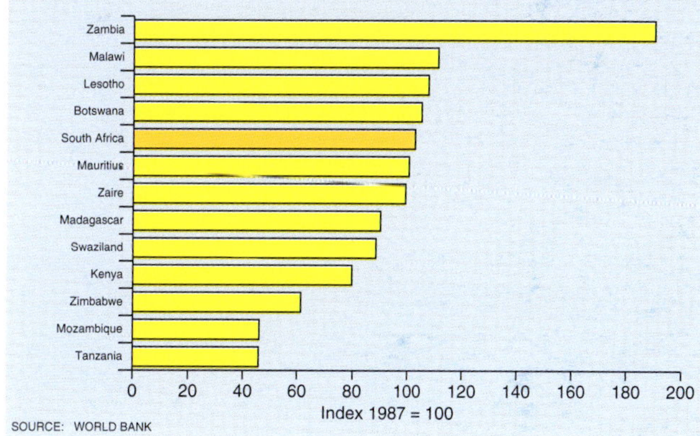

12.5 Listed companies on African stock exchanges (end 1994)

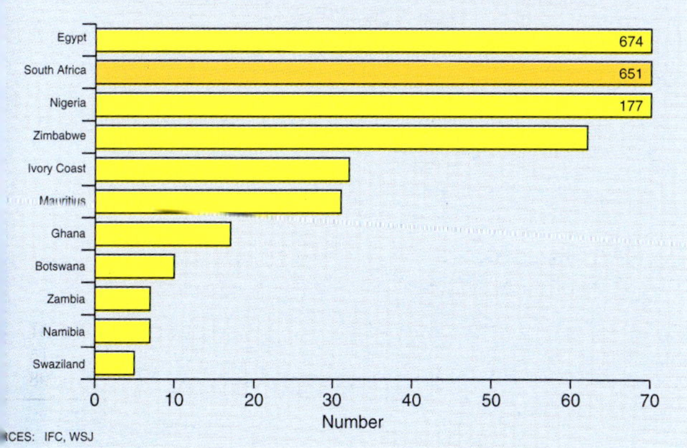

12.6 Stock exchange performance in Africa (all share index, 1993)

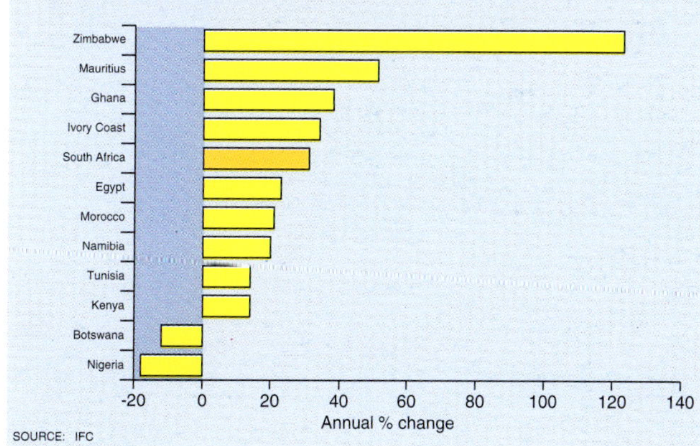

13 External sector

Mauritius achieved an average annual real export growth rate of 9,7% during 1980-92, followed by Malawi with 5,8%, Kenya with 4,1% and South Africa with only 0,7%. A decline in real exports occurred in the following countries during the same period: Zaire (-3,2%); Madagascar (-1,6%); Tanzania (-1,2%); and Zimbabwe (-0,8%).

Regarding imports, it was once again Mauritius which recorded the highest growth in real terms during 1980-92 (10,8% per annum on average), while Malawi experienced real import growth of 3,6% per annum, followed by Zimbabwe with 2,1% per annum. In South Africa real imports declined by an average 2,5% per annum during the same period, followed by Madagascar (-1,5%), Tanzania (-1,3%), Kenya (-1,0%) and Zambia (-0,7%).

Long-term capital flows varied sharply between the countries in Southern Africa. Mozambique had a net inflow of $545,7 million in 1992, followed by Zimbabwe with $472 million, Botswana with $246,5 million, Malawi with $240,9 million, Tanzania with $161,1 million, Lesotho with $43,5 million and Swaziland with $4,1 million. Regarding net capital outflow in the region in 1992, South Africa was at the top of the list ($56 million). Kenya's net outflow of long-term capital amounted to $162, million, followed by Madagascar and Mauritius with outflows of $6 million and $23,5 million respectively.

It is clearly evident from table 13.2 that commodity exports are a majo source of foreign exchange for all the countries in Southern Afric Export prices of certain commodities have increased internationally ove the years since 1980, while others have declined quite sharply, explainin to a great extent why some countries on the continent are experiencin difficult economic conditions. The price of tea in 1993 was double th in 1980, that of manganese 64% higher, that of tobacco 28% higher an that of iron ore 22% higher. Commodities that were priced lower in 19 than in 1980 were chromium (-1%), groundnuts (-3%), copper (-13% maize (-15%), bauxite (-34%), cotton (-35%), petroleum (-53%), coc (-57%), and sugar and coffee (-62%).

TABLE 13.1: BALANCE OF PAYMENTS INDICATORS AND SACU TRADE WITH SOUTHERN AFRICA

	Imports $ million 19941994	Exports $ million 1994	Trade balance $ million 1994	Balance on current account $ million 1990-93	Total reserve level $ million 1990-93	Terms of trade index 1987 = 100 1992	SACU exports % of African total 1994	SACU imports % of African total 1994
South Africa[1]	**22 280**	**25 539**	**3 259**	**1 805**	**1 019**	**104**	**..**	**..**
Kenya	1 850	1 450	-400	153	437	67	7,7	1,2
Mauritius	1 718[2]	1 333[2]	-385[2]	-93	781	102	6,3	0,6
Zimbabwe	1 575	1 775	200	-116	628	101	28,5	43,4
Tanzania	1 504	523	-981	-409	203	71	2,1	0,7
Botswana[1]	1 460	1 800	340	47	4 153	149	..	..
Angola	1 450	2 995	1 545	-995	..	98	3,6	0,8
Nambia[1]	1 126	1 327	201	142	133	95	..	..
Mozambique	989	13	-976	-317	218	..	16,3	3,9
Lesotho[1]	912[2]	134[2]	-778[2]	22	253	67	..	..
Zambia	845	1 075	230	-110	192	109	13,4	4,4
Swaziland[1]	775	343	-432	-37	264	100	..	..
Zaire	600	1 000	400	-643	55	85	4,1	15,0
Madagascar	510[2]	240[2]	-270[2]	-167	89	85	0,8	0,2
Malawi	425	350	-75	-117	62	90	7,2	7,9

[1]Member of the South African Customs Union (SACU)
[2]1993
Sources: Africa Institute, IMF, SACE, World Bank

TABLE 13.2: MAJOR PRODUCT TRADED AND TRADING PARTNER (1990-93)

	Major product traded				Major trading partner			
	Imports % of total		Exports % of total		Imports % of total		Exports % of total	
Angola	Consumer goods	40	Petroleum	90	Portugal	53	USA	64
Botswana	Consumer goods	9	Diamonds	87	South Africa	85	European Union	87
Kenya	Crude petroleum	25	Tea	25	United Arab Emirates	13	United Kingdom	18
Lesotho	Consumer goods	33	Manufactures	70	South Africa	88	European Union	35
Madagascar	Capital goods	35	Vanilla	15	France	28	France	33
Malawi	Industrial inputs and capital goods	16	Tobacco	67	South Africa	47	USA	17
Mauritius	Durable consumer goods	..	Textiles/clothing	57	France	27	Japan	25
Mozambique	Consumer goods	40	Shellfish	50	South Africa	27	Spain	29
Namibia	Capital goods	29	Diamonds and minerals	55	South Africa	90	Switzerland	35
South Africa	**Machinery and equipment**	**29**	**Gold**	**28**	**Germany**	**16**	**Switzerland**	**10**
Swaziland	Capital goods	27	Sugar	32	South Africa	94	South Africa	47
Tanzania	Consumer goods	23	Cotton	25	Saudi Arabia	11	Germany	10
Zaire	..	..	Copper	50	Belgium	23	Belgium	45
Zambia	Fertiliser	..	Copper	82	South Africa	22	Japan	18
Zimbabwe	Capital goods	41	Tobacco	29	South Africa	24	South Africa	14

Sources: Africa Institute, EIU, Financial Times, SACE, SAIIA

13.1 Merchandise imports
(1990 – 93)

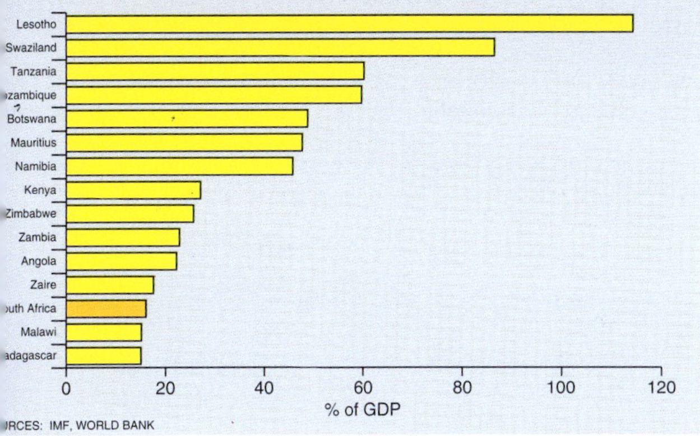

13.2 Merchandise exports
(1990 – 93)

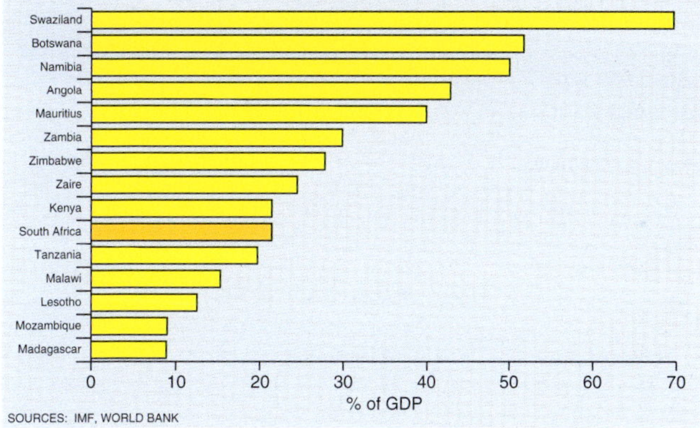

13.3 Current account balance
(1990 – 93)

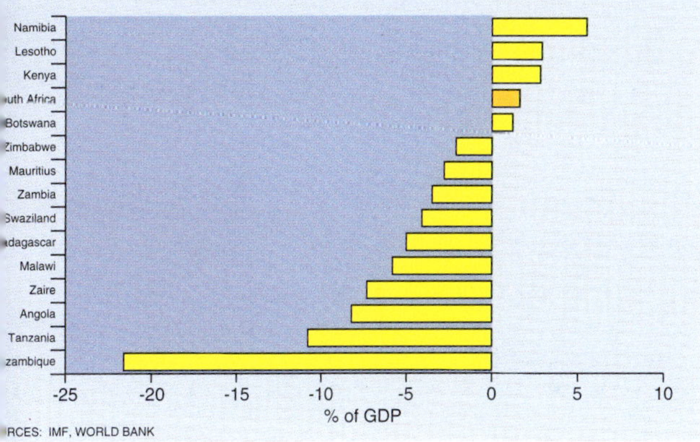

13.4 Import cover*
(1990 – 93)

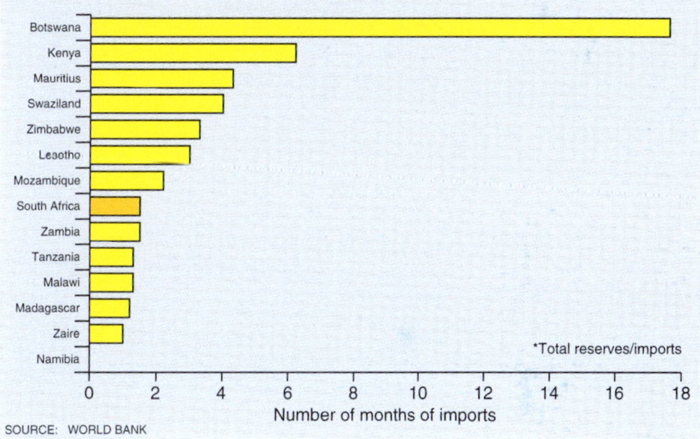

13.5 Terms of trade

A. 1980 – 85

B. 1986 – 92

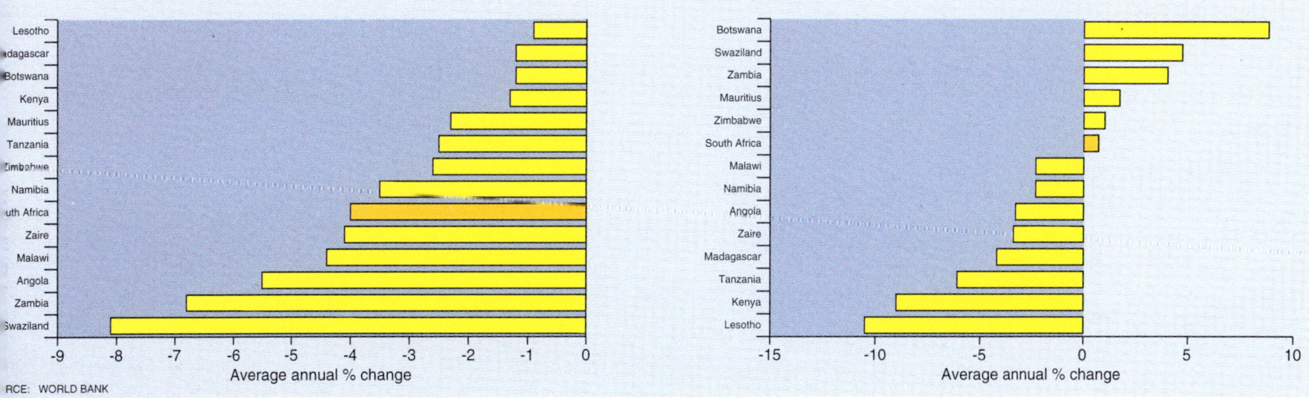

14 Foreign debt, development aid and creditworthiness

The total amount of outstanding foreign debt of the 15 Southern African countries was $86,4 billion in 1993, with South Africa accounting for 29,5%. Although South Africa's amount of foreign debt is the largest in the region, its debt ratios are among the lowest in the region (see table 14.1). This results from financial sanctions against the country and limited access to international capital markets during the second half of the 1980s and the early 1990s.

The net disbursement of total official development assistance to 14 African Development Bank (ADB) member countries in Southern Africa (see graph 14.1) amounted to $7,6 billion, ie 32% of a total of $23,7 billion for the whole of Africa. In 1988 it was $5,3 billion, or 32,7% of Africa's total of $16,2 billion in that year. At the end of 1994, about $1,3 billion of development grant aid was pledged to South Africa by 16 industrial countries worldwide, to be provided during 1994-2000.

Three international rating agencies, assigning credit ratings to developing countries, evaluated South Africa in 1994 for the first time. Th International Banking Credit Association (IBCA) gave the country a B rating, the same as that given by Standard & Poor's. This put South Afric in the same league as Argentina, Hungary, India, Mexico, the Philippin and Uruguay. Moody's gave South Africa a Baa3-rating, placing it with Chil the Czech Republic, Greece and Indonesia. These ratings indicate th South Africa is regarded as a speculative to medium investment grac country.

Country credit ratings, as calculated by *Institutional Investor*, are given i table 14.1. The global average, calculated for 135 countries worldwide, w 38,1 out of a possible score of 100 in March 1995. The average rating fc Africa (34 countries) was only 21,5, well below the global average. Souther Africa (12 countries only) achieved an average credit rating of 25, just abov the African average, but well below the global average of 38,1.

TABLE 14.1: DEBT, DEVELOPMENT AID AND CREDITWORTHINESS INDICATORS

	Foreign debt (1993)				IMF account (end March 1995)			Official development assistance	Country credit (March 1995)	
	Total $ million	Debt/GNP %	Debt/exports %	Total debt service/exports %	Quota $ million	Reserve position $ million	Credit and loans outstanding $ million	% of GDP 1992	Global ranking	Rating %
South Africa	**25 521**	**21,6**	**88,5**	**9,7**	**2 130,7**	**0,2**	**958,8**	..	**50**	**42,5**
Zaire	11 280	111,9[1]	444,7[2]	15,1[2]	454,1	–	510,8	3,4	132	7,0
Angola	9 655	84,9[2]	336,6	5,3	323,5	–	–	3,9	122	10,9
Tanzania	7 522	298,4	1 218,8	25,1	229,2	15,6	227,1	57,4	110	15,5
Kenya	6 994	135,2	300,2	28,0	311,0	19,2	428,2	11,1	84	24,9
Zambia	6 788	231,9	638,0	32,8	421,8	–	860,1	27,1	115	14,6
Mozambique	5 263	419,2	1 416,4	20,6	131,1	–	225,3	139,9	121	12,6
Madagascar	4 594	142,6	949,0	14,3	141,1	–	88,8	13,1	..	..
Zimbabwe	4 168	78,5	214,8	32,3	407,8	0,2	483,8	15,8	67	30,7
Malawi	1 821	91,5	541,0	22,1	79,4	3,4	115,6	34,5	99	18,8
Mauritius	999	30,5	46,8	6,0	114,4	11,4	–	1,8	47	45,4
Botswana	674	18,8	26,4[3]	3,6	57,1	31,7	–	3,1	42	48,5
Lesotho	512	41,8	88,5	5,5	37,3	5,5	42,6	24,5	..	..
Namibia	362[4]	14,5[4]	24,5[4]	..	155,4	–	–	5,8	..	..
Swaziland	226	25,3	36,1	3,8	57,0	4,7	–	5,4	72	28,5

[1]1989; [2]1990; [3]1991; [4]1992

Sources: ADB, Africa Institute, IMF, Institutional Investor, SARB, World Bank

TABLE 14.2: INSTITUTIONAL LENDING TO SOUTHERN AFRICAN COUNTRIES (1993)

World Bank		African Development Bank Group	
	$ million		$ million
Tanzania	340,7	Zimbabwe	116,9
Zambia	194,4	Mozambique	90,1
Zimbabwe	189,5	Malawi	80,3
Mozambique	122,9	Kenya	55,9
Kenya	114,8	Tanzania	38,3
Malawi	76,7	Swaziland	14,1
Madagascar	32,7	Namibia	12,7
Mauritius	20,0	Mauritius	2,8
Angola	8,2	Zambia	1,9
		Madagascar	0,9
Total Southern Africa	1 099,9	Total Southern Africa	413,9
Rest of sub-Saharan Africa	1 717,4	Rest of sub-Saharan Africa	989,2
Total sub-Saharan Africa	2 817,3	Total sub-Saharan Africa	1 403,1

Sources: ADB, Africa Institute

14.1 Official development assistance to ADB member countries (1992)

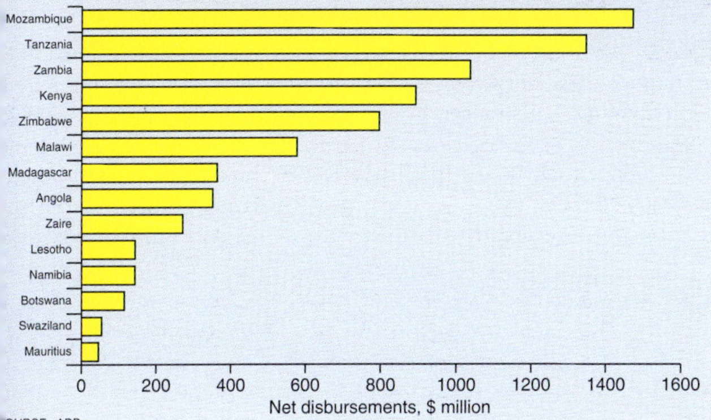

SOURCE: ADB

14.2 IMF credit and loans outstanding (end March 1995)

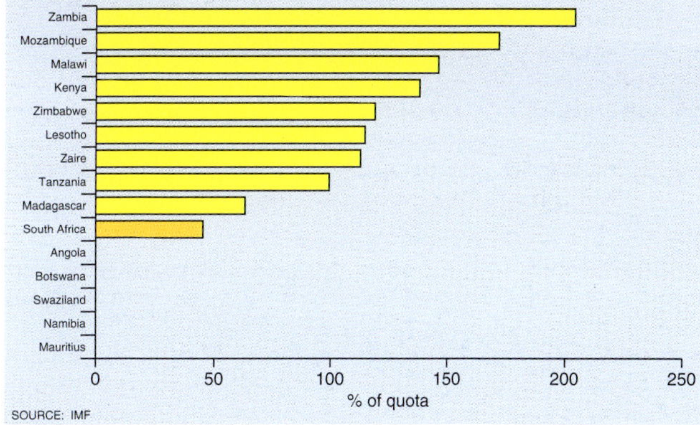

SOURCE: IMF

14.3 Interest payments on foreign debt (1993)

A. % of GNP

B. % of exports

SOURCES: AFRICA INSTITUTE, SARB, WORLD BANK

14.4 Country credit rating (March 1995)

A. Six-month change

B. One-year change

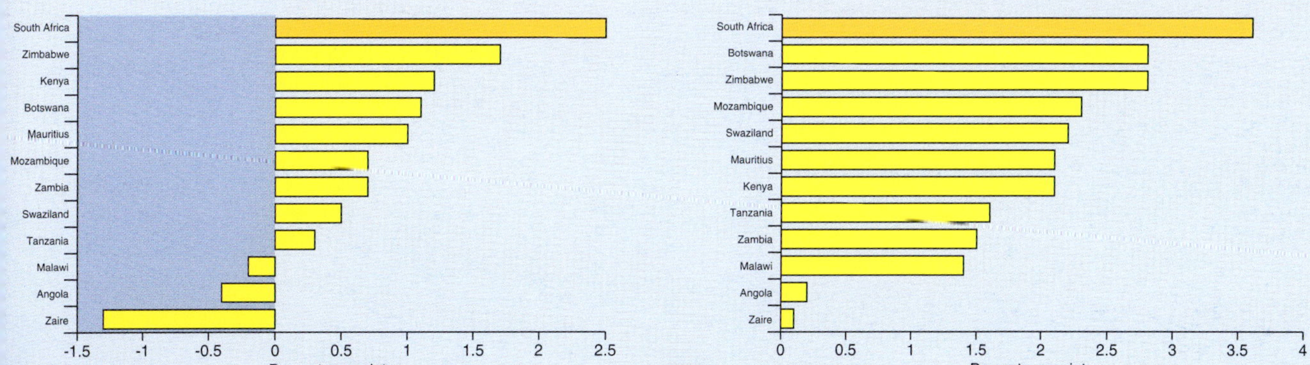

SOURCE: INSTITUTIONAL INVESTOR

15 Natural resources and environmental aspects

Most countries in Southern Africa have vast reserves of a variety of metals and minerals (see table 15.1). Metal and mineral production is an important source of income and employment in these countries. South Africa's prominence regarding metal and mineral reserves and production in the region is particularly noticeable. Gold is still the country's most important export product, comprising about 25% of total exports, but well down on the 50% in 1980.

Madagascar lost as much as 75% of its total forest habitat during the 1980s, and Zambia lost about 30%. A loss of about 46% occurred in the case of South Africa. Comparative figures for the other countries in the region vary from 40% for Tanzania to 71% for Kenya.

Almost 87% of South Africa's carbon dioxide (CO_2) emissions from industrial processes in 1991 (see graph 15.4A) came from burning solid fuels such as coal. The country's total CO_2 emissions in 1991 constituted 41,5% of that of Africa, followed by Zimbabwe with 2,5%. CO_2 emissions from the other countries in the region were in each case less than 1% of that in Africa. Chlorofluorocarbon (CFC) emissions in South Africa amounted to 41,7% of that of Africa in 1991, with the other countries in the region again at very low levels or having almost no CFC emissions. South Africa's relatively high levels of CO_2 and CFC emissions mainly result from the country's large industrial sector compared with other African countries.

TABLE 15.1: METAL AND MINERAL RESOURCES (1992-93)

Metal/mineral	Rank in Africa and percentage of world reserves						Rank in Africa and percentage of world production					
	1		2		3		1		2		3	
Diamonds	Zaire	..	**South Africa**	**..**	Botswana	..	Botswana	16,0	Zaire	14,0	**South Africa**	**10,0**
Gold	**South Africa**	**39,0**	Ghana	1,0	Zimbabwe	–	**South Africa**	**27,0**	Ghana	2,0	Zimbabwe	1,0
Platinum	**South Africa**	**88,0**	Zimbabwe	–	–	–	**South Africa**	**54,0**	Zimbabwe	–	–	–
Coal	**South Africa**	**10,0**	–	–	–	–	**South Africa**	**5,0**	Zimbabwe	–	Egypt	–
Uranium	Niger	20,0	**South Africa**	**8,0**	Namibia	5,0	Niger	8,0	Namibia	5,0	**South Africa**	**5,0**
Chromium	**South Africa**	**72,0**	Zimbabwe	21,0	Madagascar	–	**South Africa**	**33,0**	Zimbabwe	3,0	Madagascar	–
Cobalt	Zaire	28,0	Zambia	6,0	**South Africa**	**–**	Zambia	28,0	Zaire	23,0	Morocco	–
Iron ore	**South Africa**	**6,0**	Algeria	–	Mauritania	–	**South Africa**	**3,0**	Mauritania	1,0	Egypt	–
Manganese	**South Africa**	**83,0**	Gabon	3,0	Ghana	–	**South Africa**	**12,0**	Gabon	8,0	Ghana	1,0
Vanadium	**South Africa**	**45,0**	–	–	–	–	**South Africa**	**46,0**	–	–	–	–
Copper	Zambia	6,0	Zaire	5,0	**South Africa**	**2,0**	Zambia	5,0	**South Africa**	**2,0**	Zaire	1,0
Lead	**South Africa**	**4,0**	Morocco	–	Namibia	–	**South Africa**	**4,0**	Morocco	3,0	Namibia	–
Nickel	**South Africa**	**10,0**	Botswana	–	Zimbabwe	–	**South Africa**	**4,0**	Botswana	2,0	Zimbabwe	1,0
Phosphates	Morocco	64,0	**South Africa**	**7,0**	Tunisia	–	Morocco	13,0	Tunisia	4,0	**South Africa**	**2,0**
Titanium	**South Africa**	**11,0**	Sierra Leone	2,0	–	–	**South Africa**	**21,0**	Sierra Leone	5,0	–	–

Source: Africa Institute

TABLE 15.2: WATER AND FOREST RESOURCES AND ENVIRONMENTAL INDICATORS

	Freshwater resources 1987		Exploitable hydro-electric potential MW 1990	Forest area '000 km²		Protected areas 1993		Threatened species 1993		
	Total annual renewable km³	Annual with-drawals % of total		Total 1990	Annual defores-tation 1981-90	Number	'000 ha	Mammals % of total	Birds % of total	Higher order plants % of total
Zaire	1 019	0,1	530 000	1 133	7,3	8	9 917	7,5	2,5	0,1
Angola	158	0,3	100 000	231	1,7	5	2 641	5,1	1,4	0,4
Zambia	96	0,4	309 009	323	3,6	20	6 361	4,4	1,4	0,1
Tanzania	76	0,7	20 000	336	4,4	28	13 000	9,8	2,6	1,6
Mozambique	58	1,4	72 000	173	1,4	1	2	5,6	1,7	1,6
South Africa	**50**	**29,4**	**..**	**45**	**-0,4**[1]	**235**	**7 413**	**10,1**	**1,7**	**4,3**
Madagascar	40	40,8	23 061	158	1,3	36	1 115	47,6	11,2	1,7
Zimbabwe	23	5,2	19 281	89	0,6	25	3 068	4,6	0,9	2,1
Botswana	18	0,6	1	143	0,8	9	10 225	5,8	1,1	..
Kenya	15	7,3	30 000	12	0,1	36	3 470	5,5	1,7	2,3
Malawi	9	2,2	6 000	35	0,5	9	1 059	5,2	1,1	1,6
Namibia	9	1,1	1 060	126	0,4	11	10 371	7,1	1,1	0,6
Swaziland	7	4,3	400	..	..	4	46	–	1,3	1,5
Lesotho	4	2,5	2 000	..	..	1	7	6,1	2,4	0,4
Mauritius	2	20,0	65	1	–	–	–	..	9,8	27,9

[1]Increase in forest area
Source: World Bank

15.1 Freshwater resources (1987)

A. Per capita withdrawals (m^3)

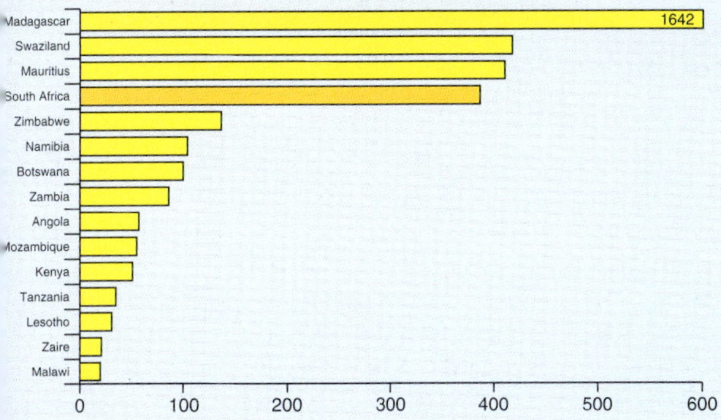

URCE: WORLD BANK

B. Sectoral withdrawals (%)

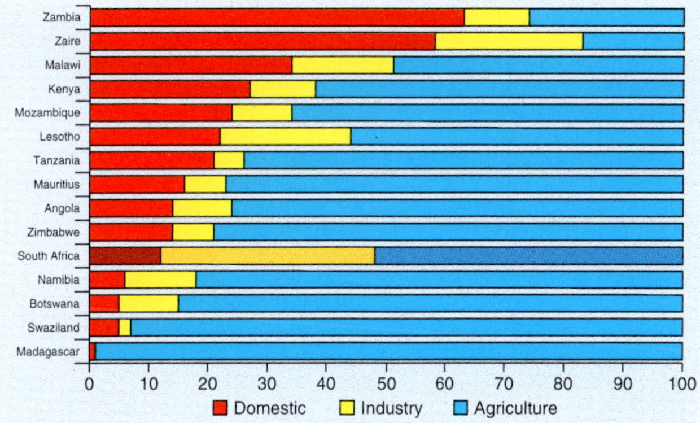

15.2 Human disturbance of nature

(% of land area, 1993)

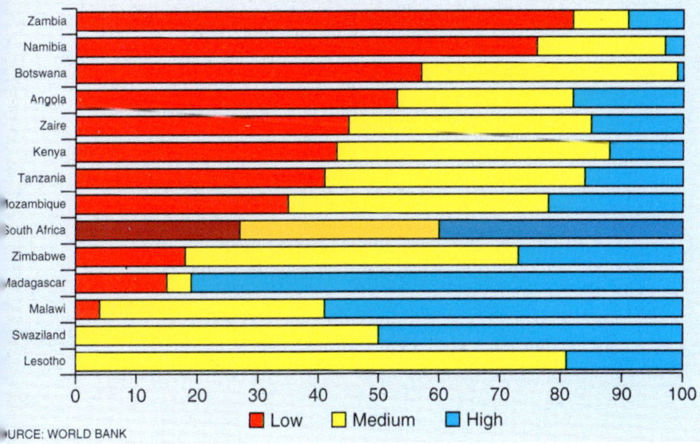

URCE: WORLD BANK

15.3 Protected areas

(% of land area, 1993)

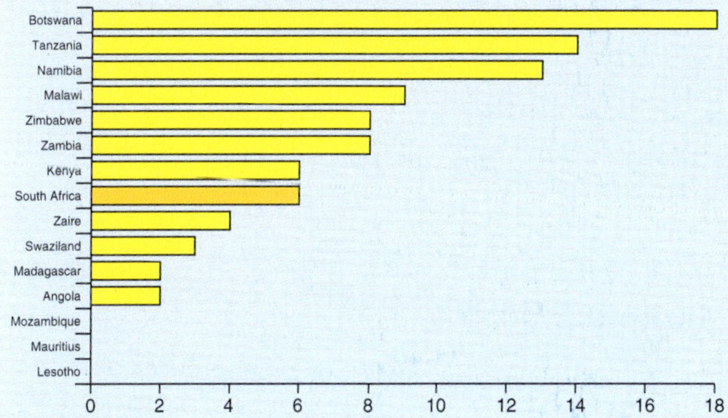

SOURCE: WORLD BANK

15.4 Carbon dioxide emissions (1991)

A. Total

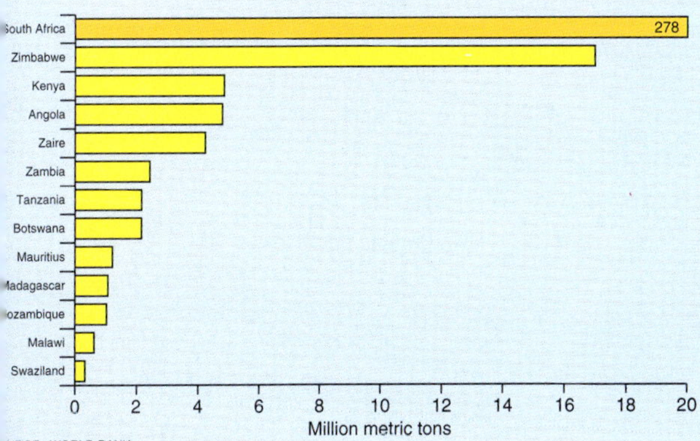

URCE: WORLD BANK

B. Per capita

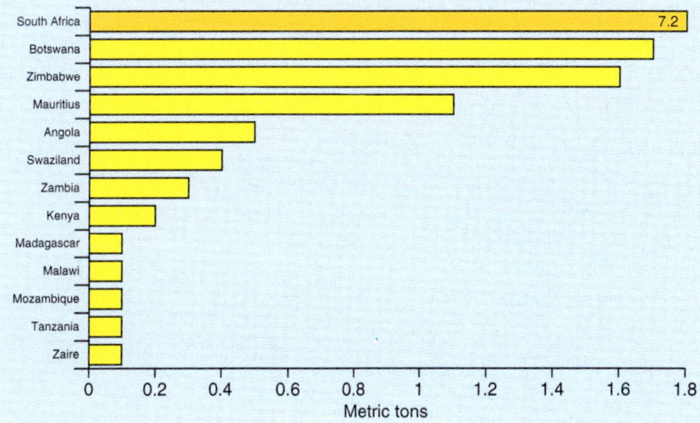

Abbreviations

ADB	African Development Bank
AIDS	Acquired Immune Deficiency Syndrome
EIU	Economist Intelligence Unit
Eskom	Electricity Supply Commission
GDE	Gross domestic expenditure
GDI	Gross domestic investment (gross domestic fixed investment plus increases/decreases in inventories)
GDP	Gross domestic product
GNP	Gross national product
GWh	Gigawatt-hour (1 000 000 units)
G7	Group of Seven industrial countries
ha	hectare
IFC	International Finance Corporation
IFR	Institute for Futures Research
IMF	International Monetary Fund
Iscor	South African Iron and Steel Corporation
km	kilometre
km^2	square kilometre
km^3	cubic kilometre
kWh	kilowatt-hour (1 unit)
m^3	cubic metre
MW	megawatt
PE	Port Elizabeth
PM	Prime Minister
Pres	President
SACE	South African Customs and Excise
SACU	South African Customs Union
SADC	Southern African Development Community
SAIIA	South African Institute of International Affairs
SARB	South African Reserve Bank
Sasol	South African Coal, Oil and Gas Corporation
t	metric ton
UN	United Nations
WSJ	Wall Street Journal

ADCORP GRAPHICS